P9-EMK-089

First-Time
Europe

A ROUGH GUIDE SPECIAL

CREDITS

Editorial: Andrew Rosenberg, Martin Dunford
Production: Susanne Hillen, Nicola Williamson
Design and lay-out: Henry Iles
Maps: Melissa Flack, David Callier, Matt Welton
Proofreading: Eric Wechter
Index: Peter Schmidt

Acknowledgments
In this second edition, I wish to thank Elaine Petrocelli for her unfailing support, generosity, and encouragement over the past year. Every author should have such a patron and friend. I also wish to thank Sheila Damiani and her family for their kindness and hospitality during my time as their guest in Naples. Finally, this edition, and all subsequent editions, are dedicated to Celine Elise Johansen, for the very best of reasons.

The author would like to thank the following people for their assistance with the first edition: Joanne Palamountain, for her editing and encouragement; Steve Welter, for the same reasons; Jennifer Rankin, for testing a half-complete manuscript in Europe; Robert O. Ritchie and Scott Belliveau, for their early support of my writing career; Larry Bennett, for unbiased, positive comments at just the right time; Joanie and Guillaume Cre'te', for too many things to mention; Bruce Kuyper, scobe-at-law, for his legal wizardry; Jim Martin, for the generous donation of his time and expertise; and the dozens of travelers who shared their opinions, and the hundreds of Europeans who made me feel welcome in their countries. To all of you: Thank you.

This second edition published 1997 by Rough Guides Ltd
    1 Mercer St, London WC2H 9QJ
    375 Hudson Street, New York 10014
    Internet: mail@roughtravl.co.uk

Distributed by The Penguin Group
    Penguin Books Ltd, 27 Wrights Lane, London W8 5TZ
    Penguin Books USA Inc., 375 Hudson Street, New York 10014
    Penguin Books Canada Ltd, 10 Alcorn Avenue, Toronto, Ontario MV4 1E4
    Penguin Books Australia Ltd, PO Box 257, Ringwood, Victoria 3134
    Penguin Books (NZ) Ltd, 182–190 Wairau Road, Auckland 10

Printed in the United States

The publishers and author have done their best to ensure the accuracy and currency of all information in First-Time Europe; however, they can accept no responsibility for any loss or inconvenience sustained by any reader as a result of its information or advice.

No part of this book may be reproduced in any form without permission from the publisher except for the quotation of brief passages in reviews.

© Louis CasaBianca, 1996, 1997

256 pages; includes index
A catalogue record for this book is available from the British Library
ISBN 1-85828-270-5

First-Time
Europe

A ROUGH GUIDE SPECIAL

Written by

Louis CasaBianca

with illustrations by

Jerry Swaffield

CONTENTS

LIST OF MAPS

DEDICATION

John Wesley Hardin was an outlaw, thief, and gunslinger in the American Old West. Whatever his other failings, Mr. Hardin performed one act which every budget traveler has dreamed of doing: he shot a man for snoring too loudly. In many a crowded hostel dorm room, and in many a thin-walled pension, many a desperate, bleary-eyed traveler has found solace in the memory of Mr. Hardin's act. In recognition of John Wesley Hardin's role as patron spirit of the snore-oppressed, this book is dedicated to his memory.

INTRODUCTION

This is the second edition of *First-Time Europe*, the first edition of which was very kindly received by travelers in the United States and Canada. New information has been included for those traveling to Europe from Australia, New Zealand, and Britain; and the entire text has been reviewed and updated. More information for older travelers and for those with slightly larger budgets has also been added.

These aspects of *First-Time Europe* have changed, but the main focus has not. This book is designed to help the first (or second, or third) time European traveler plan and complete a safe, rewarding, enjoyable, and affordable trip. It truly is: "What you need to know before you go." So, as you read these words and consider going to Europe and buying this book, I can say two things with confidence: (1) Go to Europe; you will have the most broadening, rewarding, and educational experience of your life. (2) This little book can help you tremendously, both before and during your trip. If you can come up with about two thousand dollars, I can get you to Europe for a month or more. You won't regret buying this book, I promise. See you in Europe.

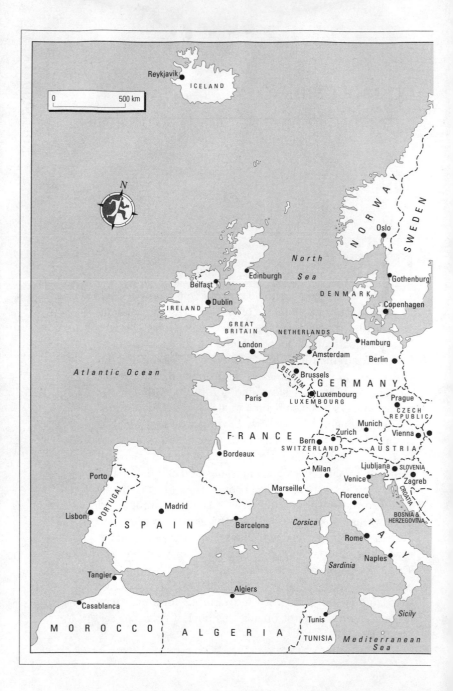

EUROPE

F I N L A N D

Helsinki

St Petersburg

Stockholm

Tallinn

ESTONIA

Baltic Sea

Riga

LATVIA

Moscow

LITHUANIA

R U S S I A

KALININGRAD

Vilnius

Minsk

P O L A N D

BELARUS

Warsaw

Kiev

Krakow

U K R A I N E

SLOVAKIA

Bratislava

Chisinau

Budapest

MOLDOVA

HUNGARY

R O M A N I A

Bucharest

GEORGIA

T'bilisi

Baku

Belgrade

Black Sea

AZERBAIJAN

SERBIA

ARMENIA

MONTENEGRO

BULGARIA

Yerevan

Sofia

AZERB.

MACEDONIA

İstanbul

I R A N

ALBANIA

Ankara

Tirana

GREECE

T U R K E Y

İzmir

Athens

Baghdad

Crete

CYPRUS

S Y R I A

Beirut

I R A Q

LEBANON

CHAPTER ONE

WHY GO TO EUROPE?

Every year thousands of people head to Europe for the first time, and I'd guess all of them want the best trip they can get for the money. This book is intended to help someone taking one of those trips see Europe as cheaply and as enjoyably as possible. The first time I traveled to Europe I just picked up and went, and had to learn the hard way. That trip was a wonderful experience, but it would have been much easier, and certainly less expensive, if someone who had been there before had given me his or her advice. Now, several years and much European travel later, this book contains the advice I give to friends before their first trip.

I know you're at least thinking about going to Europe, or else you wouldn't be reading this book. So the very first and most important piece of advice I can give you is one word: GO! If you have the time, and can find the money somewhere, anywhere, just GO! You will not regret it, I promise you. When you walk into St Peter's in Rome and look down a central aisle longer than two football fields, over the spot where Charlemagne was crowned twelve centuries ago, and then give a glance to the right and see Michelangelo's *Pieta,* you will not regret going. When you sit on a beach in the Greek Islands and watch the sun set into the Aegean Sea, and listen to the others on that beach laughing and chatting in six languages as the ouzo and wine get passed around, you will not regret the time and money it took to get there. When you wake up in Paris and have a choice between going to the Eiffel Tower, or the Louvre, or Versailles, or Notre Dame, or the Cathedral at Chartres, or a dozen other wonders only a walk or a train ride away, your trip will seem very cheap indeed. That's not to say that you shouldn't try to go as inexpensively as possible; in fact, this book is written in large part to help you do just that. But later in life, when you look back two or five years on, and ask yourself whether it was worth it to go when you did, I promise you the answer will be "Yes." If you have the time and the money, do it. If you have the time, but think you don't have the money, keep reading, and maybe I can show you that Europe for a few weeks, or for a summer, can be a lot cheaper than you think.

And, if the whole process of going seems like too much of a bother, too much planning and time, remember the following: By spending a summer in Europe you will visit countries that are both much older and very different from your own, and gain a new perspective on your own country as a result. You will meet people who happily live lives very different from your own. And you will see some of the greatest creations of the human mind and spirit: legendary wonders of art and architecture that form a large part of the collective heritage of the human race. That's why you're going to Europe, not to hunt for the cheapest hostel or the best rate of exchange. Remember this during all the dry talk about money and packs and all that practical stuff.

Why Go Cheaply?

As recently as ten years ago, seeing Europe by staying in hostels or small hotels and using a Eurail train pass was pretty much a student option. No longer. Savvy travelers have recognized the rewards of such a trip in comparison with a much more expensive tour. Because of this, although I am speaking mainly to college students, recent graduates, and teachers who are planning budget trips for several weeks, the advice in this book should be useful for independent travelers of all ages. If indeed you are an "older traveler" finally getting to go to Europe for the first time, or someone who's going back after having served there in World War II, I would like to add a special farewell. To those who are now realizing that European trip they have dreamed of, congratulations. I hope it's the best trip of your life.

This book can also help those who are not lucky enough to have an entire summer to spend on the road. Travelers with larger budgets who want to avoid bland hotels and crowded tours may also find the information contained here very useful. If you do plan on taking a tour, I promise that this book will still serve as a worthwhile introduction and reference.

This is not a guidebook. There are plenty of excellent guides available to every conceivable region of Europe. This book is about the nuts and bolts of travel, especially with regard to planning, saving money, and getting the most out of a trip. I can't guarantee that everything in this book is right for every traveler; after all, my advice reflects primarily my own experiences. But I can promise that I will help the first-time traveler avoid some very common mistakes and frustrations, save time and money, and skip the sometimes painful learning process I went through. This is the book I needed and couldn't find before I left on my first trip. I hope you find it helpful on yours.

(Note: All prices listed in this book are in US dollars unless otherwise noted.)

CHAPTER TWO

PLANNING YOUR TRIP

Calvin Coolidge once said that if you look up the road and see ten troubles coming toward you, nine of them are going to run off the road before they get to you. That's the attitude to have in planning and getting ready for a trip to Europe. Remember, tens of thousands of people just like you went to Europe last year and had a great time. So will you. Plan, but don't overplan. Prepare, but don't stress out over every detail. To be honest, if you were to throw away this book, pack a tote bag, and hit the airport tomorrow, you could probably go and have a great time. With some planning and advice, though, you could have a much better time for about half the price. You're way ahead of the game by buying this book, so relax. I've made all the mistakes already, and you get to hear about them now instead of repeating them.

Your Passport – First Things First

This is an absolute essential – you won't be allowed on the plane without one. If you don't have a passport, send away for one as soon as possible. *Don't put this off.* To get an American passport, you will need (1) your birth certificate or some other proof of birth; (2) proof of identity (like a driver's license) with a signature; (3) an application form, available at any large post office, court house or passport office; and (4) two photos that are described on the form. Passport agencies, listed in the phone book under "Federal Government, Department of State," are located in twelve major cities. If you don't have a copy of your birth certificate, send away for it *immediately* – the process can take a while, and until you have your birth certificate or other proof in hand, you can't apply for a passport. Other forms of proof, such as certificates of baptism, are described in detail on the form.

Passports are good for ten years (five if you're under 18) and cost a very rude $65 ($40 for those under 18). Figure that into your budget. If you already have a passport, note that some countries require a passport to be valid for a certain amount of time *after* you enter that country. If your passport is going to expire within six months of the beginning of your trip it's probably worth renewing it. In any case you should know that you'll be nailed for $100 if you return to the States with an expired passport.

Seriously, if you don't have a passport and especially if you don't have your birth certificate handy, the best thing you can do is put down this book right now and start the process immediately. As you might expect, there is a flood of applications every spring. During the height of the summer, well after the peak application period, there can still be as much as a five-week processing wait. Other times of the year it may take six weeks, or five days, or three weeks. The moral of this story is pretty obvious: Get yours now.

PASSPORT CONTROL

Expedited Passports

If you are panicking as you read this because you have a thousand dollars' worth of nonrefundable airline tickets for next week and no passport, take heart. For some extra money (a $30 surcharge), you can get a passport expedited, if and only if you can prove – with plane tickets or confirmed reservations – that you are leaving within ten days. You can apply for an expedited passport from a passport agency, a post office, or direct to Passport Lockbox, PO Box 371971, Pittsburgh, PA 15250-7971; clearly mark the envelope "EXPEDITE," and be sure to include the usual fees, plus the surcharge fee, and proof of imminent departure. Expedited passports will be processed within three business days of receipt by a passport agency; if this deadline cannot be met, the expedite fee will be refunded.

There is a bit of a "black hole" in this whole process. You can't apply for the expedited service until ten days before your trip; and I wouldn't apply through the regular process if I was within about four weeks of my departure. So from four weeks until ten days prior to your trip, you must sweat it out until you can send an expedited application. The moral, as before, is Get It Now!

Canadian passports

The Canadian government maintains passport offices in most major cities, and encourages citizens to apply in person. Application forms are available from post offices and some travel agents. The application should be submitted with two identical passport-sized photos, proof of citizenship (again a birth certificate is best), and the fee of Can$35; passports are valid for five years. In theory the passport will be ready within five working days. For more information, call ✆ 1-800-567-6868.

British passports

Application forms can be obtained at post offices; depending on the time of year, the turn-around after posting the form can be up to six weeks. Although the

London office will process applications in a day, it may be a very long day of waiting and queues. Cost is £20; passports are valid for ten years. For more information, and the phone numbers of the various British passport offices, call © 0990-210410.

Australian passports

Aussies can pick up an application at a post office or passport office. Passport offices are located in all major cities. After filling out the form (which will take some time), you must appear back in person at a post office or passport office – it may be necessary to make an appointment. Expect a cost of Aus$120 (children Aus$60) and a turnaround of three weeks or so. Call toll-free © 131-232 if you have questions.

New Zealand passports

New Zealanders can obtain an application form from a travel agent, then just follow the instructions. The price is NZ$80 (children NZ$40), and you should have your passport within fifteen days of posting the application; it's good for ten years. If you have any questions contact the Department of Internal Affairs at © (04) 474-8100.

Visas

A visa is a special notation, stamped or glued into your passport, that allows you to enter and exit a country. Something like: "Bearer is hereby granted leave to travel in Elbonia from June 1, 1997 – August 30, 1997, for the purpose of tourism."

Visas are an unfortunate holdover from the days when European borders meant something. Today, they are little more than bureaucratic inconveniences, and some can be surprisingly expensive to obtain, especially for Canadians. Fortunately, very few Western European countries still require them, and fewer Eastern European countries do each passing year. See *Basics* #1 for more on visas.

Planning

The first thing to do in any serious planning is to get an overview. This part is easy and fun. Just find a large map of Europe and let your imagination loose. Paris? The Norwegian fjords? Liters of beer in Munich? The nightlife in Amsterdam? Prague, and the Charles Bridge? Pubbing and clubbing in London? The ruins of Pompeii? The midnight sun in Sweden? One country for a month, or the highlights of five different nations? Get an atlas or a large map that covers all of Europe, and some coffee table books from the library, and wander at will. One of the true joys of travel is seeing for yourself a place that, in photographs, looks too exotic and beautiful to be real. To get some of those pictures, look for books called *Insight Guides* at the library. These books have great photographs but are not very useful for traveling. Also, *National Geographic*, at one time or another, has published a story on just about every place in Europe. Most libraries also have video collections that include documentaries and/or tourist office productions about Europe. Take notes on any place that appeals to you.

The next step is a bit harder – deciding what you want to see, and how best to arrange your trip to see it all. The most common entry and exit points

to and from Europe are London, Paris, Frankfurt, and Milan, and it is generally cheapest to fly in and out of those cities (see Chapter 5 for more on this). Spend some time thinking about it, with the help of the resources below. Once you have a rough list of what's important to you, and a rough itinerary, you can start thinking about when and how to get there. When you're doing your planning, don't plan too rigidly. When you get to Europe you will hear of places, meet people, and find out about events that may cause you to change your plans. Leave some days open so you can do this along the way.

A word of advice about how *much to* plan to see. A typical list of the "must-see cities" might include London, Paris, Rome, Florence, Venice, Prague, Amsterdam, Munich, Berlin, Madrid, and Vienna. But notice that if you were to spend a week in each place – and allow, say, twelve days for moving around – you'd have to spend from June 1 through August 28 in Europe to visit them all. You would also miss Greece, Ireland, Scandinavia, Scotland, and Switzerland completely, be wretchedly sick of traveling by the second month, and arrive home totally exhausted.

The point is this: You can't see all of Europe in one summer, and it's not even fun to try. Remember, you only get one chance to see a place for the first time, when everything is fresh and new. The first time you see Paris, give it the week or so that it deserves. Going there for a day will simply be unsatisfying and will inevitably diminish the experience the second time you go. I'm not one of those snobs who claims you have to spend weeks in a place to really say that you've been there. I am saying, however, that if you try to do and see too much your trip will become a blur of trains, hostels, museums, paintings, and churches that all run together after a while. Plan realistically. Figure out what is really important to you, go see those cities or things at a reasonable pace, and don't get caught up in the "I've got to complete my list" syndrome. If this is going to be your only trip for a long time, it's understandable that you want to see as much as possible.

But when you're in Europe, if you ever feel you *have* to go sightseeing, rather than you *get* to go sightseeing, you're pushing too hard. Take a break at this point. Planning to visit a beach resort about halfway through your trip is a good idea if you think you might need a bit of a rest.

National Tourist Offices

This is another one of the fun parts. Just call or write the national tourist offices listed in *Basics #3* and in a few days your mailbox is miraculously full of brochures. Their heavy, glossy pages are covered with pictures of beautiful sights and happy, smiling people. Even a toxic waste dump would look like heaven in one of these.

This type of information is good for getting a first glimpse of a country, and especially for revealing places, sights, or monuments you may never have heard of. When you call tourist offices, let them know your intended budget and your specific areas of interest. Ask for maps, since good maps can be expensive and tourist office maps are sometimes of surprisingly high quality. Maps of entire countries or regions are needed to plan effectively. If you have any special interest, such as long-distance walking, bicycling and so on, ask for information on that, too. Most of these places have an incredible amount of information, and most of it is free for the asking. Before leaving on your trip, copy whatever information you need out of these glossy brochures and then leave them at home – they're too heavy and awkward to carry with you.

Other Travelers

There is nothing like up-to-date firsthand information. If you know somebody who has been to Europe recently, give them the third degree. Don't take everything they say as gospel truth (or for that matter, everything *I* say); after all, you are a different person going at a different time.

But if they rave about a quiet little village you've never heard of, consider a visit. If they mention a specific hotel that was the site of a mouse convention, or the home of herds of corn-fed cockroaches, write that name down and avoid it.

When to Go

For most of us, summer is the travel season, whether we like it or not. Certainly the vast majority of students and teachers will be traveling between May 15 and September 15. The good and bad aspects of travel during the summer are obvious: The weather is nice, but the crowds are not. So for the first time (and not the last), I will repeat one of the Three Great Truths of European travel: GO EARLY. The best time to travel is in May. Spring is in the air, European students are still in school, the summer hordes have not arrived, and it's as good as it's going to get. What this means to students and teachers is that it will be worth your while to leave as soon as possible after school is out. While you shouldn't go directly from your Organic Chemistry final to the airport, don't wait around just to catch a concert on June 10 when you could have gone on May 30.

Travel quality peaks around June 1, before the tourists really start to arrive from abroad, declines steadily throughout June and July as more and more Europeans hit the trail, and then drops off a cliff in August, as millions of French, Greek, and Italian tourists, among others, go on a vacation frenzy (almost all French and Italians take their holidays during August). This means that not only beaches and major attractions are crowded, but also many shops and restaurants are closed, and others may have shorter hours. Bear in mind, too, that actually traveling at the beginning or end of August is very unpleasant, with massive traffic jams and overcrowded trains and ferries.

Weather is another factor to consider. A traveler who spends a summer in Europe can expect some very hot days and nights in southern Europe (Spain, Italy, Greece) and warm days with cool nights in most other places. Rain is possible anywhere at any time, especially in Britain, Ireland and Scandinavia, so it is advisable to bring a light rain jacket or small umbrella. Outside of the South, layered clothing is a good idea because days can include chilly mornings, hot afternoons and cool evenings. More detailed weather information, on specific countries, is best obtained from a national tourist office. Europe is a big place, and it is hard to generalize about continent-wide weather conditions.

• •

A TRAVEL-TIMING STORY

Remember what I said earlier about mistakes I made? The huge drop-off in travel quality as of August 1st was something I experienced firsthand, in the worst possible way. I made the fatal mistake of catching a ferry from Athens to the Greek Islands on August 1st. It was absolute, stinking hell on Earth. Getting on the ferry was like being in a food riot in Somalia – thousands of sweating, cursing backpackers fighting their way through trucks and cars belching unfiltered exhaust into the ferry's hold, and then inching their way up two tiny staircases to the deck, swearing and blaspheming in ten languages. Now, imagine the grungiest, seediest hotel in New York City. Imagine the floor in the lobby, covered with the stains, dirt, and cigarette butts of the last twenty years. That ferry ride, camped outside on a steel deck, was like rolling around on that floor for fifteen hours, freezing at night and roasting during the day, choked by diesel exhaust, packed cheek to jowl with hundreds of other travelers, all of whom were smoking, snoring, or drunk. On arrival at the islands, every possible form of accommodation was full to the rafters.

Needless to say, I do not recommend travel to the Greek Islands, or other vacation spots favored by Europeans, in the month of August. More on this later, but it bears repeating here. Make reservations well ahead if you will be traveling to major cities in August. Even in July reservations are a good idea.

• •

Classes and Reading

If you're thinking about a trip to Europe some time in the long term, say in six months or a year, one of the best things you can do now to prepare is to take a course in Art History, Architecture, or European History. A survey course in Art History, in particular, will vastly increase the relevance and interest of all of those paintings and statues. Most of the truly unique attractions of Europe, particularly in Italy and France, involve art and/or architecture in one form or another. Knowing even the basics about who the major artists of the various periods were, and what they are best known for, will vastly increase your enjoyment of their works. If you don't have the time or opportunity to take a course, any decent library will have several metric tons of those big glossy books on art and artists. My personal favorites are the Time-Life History of Art series – about thirty books each concentrating on one particular artist and his world. They are designed for the general population, have beautiful illustrations, and are well written. Look also for the Thames & Hudson art books: well-illustrated paperbacks, each of which covers a particular artistic or architectural style or era. In any book, if you see a painting or piece of sculpture you like, note where it is (usually written right next to the picture), then go see it when you get there. When you do, be prepared for a surprise, since what is beautiful on a page in a book is very often spectacular in real life, particularly sculptures.

No matter how much time you spend reading about art and architecture, I don't think you'll regret it. I've certainly never heard anyone say that they have. On the other hand, I've lost count of the number of times I've heard someone say, "I wish I knew more about this stuff, so it was more to me than just a bunch of paintings."

Languages

One of the most humbling experiences an American (or Australian or Kiwi) can have in Europe is to meet a teenager who speaks three or four languages. For true humiliation, spend a few minutes at the Amsterdam Visitors Bureau and watch the twenty-year-old behind the desk switch from Dutch to German to Spanish to English to French and back to Dutch again without batting an eyelash. It's almost as bad in Scandinavia, where my pitiful efforts in Danish or Swedish are usually met with "How's it going – anything I can do for you, just let me know, okay?" I know – and have used – all the excuses: The United States and Canada are huge countries, we don't have as many languages as close to us as Europeans do, and so on. Those statements are indeed true, but not much help when you're trying to function and get around in a different culture. The ability to speak a language, even a little, will add tremendously to the enjoyment of visiting a country, and will work wonders when dealing with the local residents. Even a phrasebook or dictionary, especially if you are going to be spending a long time in one country, can be very useful. See *Basics* #10 for some simple words to get you started.

By speaking the local language you're making an obvious effort to reach out, while simultaneously showing respect for the local culture, and that will be noted and appreciated. (Canadians will find their French very useful in this regard, especially if they make it known that they are from Canada.) Also, while it may be true that "everybody speaks English" in the big cities, that will not be the case out in the sticks. Even a single semester or quarter of a language, or an adult school class, is well worth taking. I know how much the moderate amount of Spanish I can speak has meant to me. I once gave my seat on a bus to an older woman in Spain, who refused to take it out of pride. When I managed to say "It's only because you look like my girlfriend" her laughter was worth all of those miserable verbs conjugated over the years. I don't know who said it, but this quote is both beautiful and appropriate:

Saber una otra lengua es tener una otra alma.
To know another language is to possess another soul.

Planning How to Get Around

Once you've got a rough idea of where you want to go and what you want to see, the next step is deciding how to get around to all those great places and things.

Planning this step is kind of a chicken-or-the-egg situation, in that you won't know what's best until you get there, but you have to plan (and buy train passes if necessary) before you leave. This next section will discuss the options available that require planning before you leave. Other options that don't require as much planning, such as hitching and ride-share, are covered in Chapter 7.

Trains

For most people budgeting their way around Europe, there is a simple answer to the transport question: Buy a train pass in some form, or just some train tickets, and hit the tracks. There are good reasons for this: European trains are generally fast, convenient, reliable and seem to go everywhere; during the summer, they are full of travelers from dozens of countries, and you can meet some very fun people. They're a great way to travel.

If you only want to see two or three cities, then you probably should buy individual train tickets between those cities, rather than a pass. If you want to go to more than four or five cities, especially if they are in different countries, then consider a train pass. The most popular kind of pass, at least for visitors from outside Europe, is the "Eurail" pass, which comes in a number of forms and covers from one to seventeen countries. These allow either unlimited travel over a period of time, or travel on a certain number of days within a given time period (say, five days within a month). You'll find more information than you thought possible on train passes and their various validities and restrictions in *Basics #2* – there's too much to put in here. Take some time with it, even though the material is a bit dry. Remember also that any good rail agent can quote you individual point-to-point ticket prices, to help you decide whether or not you need a rail pass at all. Citizens or subjects of EU countries are ineligible for Eurail passes, but get an even better deal with InterRail passes, also discussed in *Basics #2*.

WARNING: *Eurail and other train passes should be purchased before leaving for Europe.* There are a few major cities (London, for example) where *some* types of passes may be available if you can prove that you have been in Europe for less than six months, but they cost several hundred dollars more than if purchased outside of Europe. It is far easier to buy a pass before you leave. If you are already in Europe, as a student, for example, you can have a pass bought for you and sent out with a small amount of difficulty. Contact any pass vendor (listed in *Basics #2*) for specific information.

Finally, even if the train is your transportation choice, don't skip the rest of the information in this chapter. You may find a situation where some other way of getting around will work for you for a side trip, or when your pass runs out.

Airplanes

Because of their relatively high ticket prices, airplanes are best only for special cases, such as flying to remote locations that would otherwise involve lengthy and complicated travel. For example, a plane trip from London to the Greek Islands compares very favorably with the same trip by train – it costs about the same, but takes four hours as opposed to the better part of two days. This is a slightly special case, where flights are regular and cheap, and the destination is hard to get to by train and boat. However, if you are planning a long round trip to a specific destination, take the time to calculate how much it will cost you in incidental fees, time and travel days and/or train pass days. If time is short or the routing is long and complex, it just might be worth your while to fly. See Chapter 7 on "Getting Around" for more on this.

The center of cheap European flights is London, and some truly amazing deals can be found among the multitude of discount travel agencies located there. If you're thinking about going to Greece, Turkey, Israel, Egypt, or even just Spain or Portugal while on your European trip, consider flying into and out of London. If you haven't considered them, realize that you can get to those destinations for as little as $200–300 round trip.

There are a number of ways to track down these cheap flights. *Time Out*, a London magazine, always has a lot of ads for cheap flights, as does the *Evening Standard*, a London newspaper. However, perhaps the best (certainly the cheapest) sources for cheap flights are the freebie magazines, most of them geared at Australian and New Zealand travelers. They are available from self-service bins and budget accommodations all over the city, and contain ads from discount travel agencies for flights all over Europe and the world. Of these, *TNT*, specifically geared to the budget traveler, is the best. In the States or Canada, copies may be available at large bookstores or at Tower Records. Failing that, the *TNT* address is: 14–15 Child's Place, Earls Court, London, SW5 9RX, England (℗ 0171-373-3377). Send away for a copy well in advance of your trip, and see if some of the available flights fit your plans and your budget. These will change by the time you get there, but at least you will get an idea.

Also, remember that many of the best deals are last-second, stand-by, or some other wrinkle on normal air travel. If you are in London prior to flying home, you may find an incredible deal and be able spend the last week of your trip in Israel rather than in London. It's worth calling around to the discount agencies on arrival in London to check this out.

Boats and Ferries

If you are planning on taking a boat to Europe, have your butler return this book for a refund, as you don't need my advice on saving money.

While in Europe, however, there are numerous ferries, lake steamers, and riverboats for those in the mood to set sail, many of which are cheaper with a Eurail pass. These discounts are listed on the back of the free map that comes with that Eurail pass. If you're visiting the Greek Islands, you'll undoubtedly travel by ferry at some point, and you probably will if you're traveling from London to the rest of the continent (although now there's the option of the Channel Tunnel). One "cruise" line that might interest budget travelers is the Norwegian Coastal Steamer Route, or "Hurtigruten." These boats leave Bergen and arrive six days later in Kirkenes, well above the Arctic Circle, having cruised through some absolutely spectacular scenery on the way. Fares are very reasonable, especially for Norway, since these are working boats and not meant specifically for tourists. Off-season fares (from September 1 to April 30) are extremely reasonable, and anyone in Europe at this time should consider this trip. The Norwegian Tourist Board can give full details – see *Basics* #3 for their address.

Buses

Unlike the United States, where riding Greyhound is like a sentence in a mobile prison, buses in Europe are generally clean, safe, reliable, and fast. In some countries – Greece for example – express buses are faster than trains for some trips. This is also the case in Ireland, and, to a lesser extent, in England. If you plan on spending most of your time in these countries, then a train pass may not pay for itself. This is definitely so if you won't be traveling much.

If you are planning to see only major cities on your trip and you are on a very tight budget, you might want to look into *Eurobus*. This is a road-bound, abbreviated version of Eurail, with buses that travel in loops and spurs around Europe, stopping at accommodations in various cities. Note that *Eurobus* routes only take in major cities, and you will be let out at campgrounds and some of the cheaper (and more crowded) hostels. On the other hand, these buses are dirt cheap, costing as little as $300 for an under-26 two-month pass, or up to $450 for an over-26 three-month pass. The number for *Eurobus*'s agent in the States is © 1-800-EUROBUS; in London the number is © 0181-991-1021.

Another bus option worth considering is the "slow coach" operation. These are also designed for ultra-budget types, and consist of a number of buses that follow a pre-set route around a country, dropping off and picking up travelers anywhere along the route. You buy a ticket for a certain time, then jump on and off buses as desired. Be advised that these operations focus on the cheapest possible accommodations when they stop for the night. Check the London magazines previously mentioned or at tourist offices in major European cities.

Finally, if you are planning only a few trips between cities, say three weeks in London, followed by three weeks in Paris, followed by three weeks back in London, making those trips by bus is going to be your cheapest option. You certainly don't need a rail pass for such a trip.

Cars

A car is best for getting to out-of-the-way towns the train doesn't go to, and for seeing the truly rural parts of a country. Towns and villages without train stations, at least those some distance from big cities and the highways, are bound to be quieter, more traditional, and see far fewer foreign tourists than rail towns do. I have traveled in some very out-of-the-way places, in both Europe and the Middle

East, and the people were generally more friendly (or curious) and certainly less jaded. When little kids follow you around staring, you've come to an unspoiled place. The downside is that traveling by car can insulate you from your surroundings: You don't meet people in the same way you do getting around by train, and you can end up feeling as if you're traveling in a bit of a vacuum.

A FEW WORDS ABOUT TOURS

There is a tendency among travelers to look down on tours, as if it's "wrong" to see Europe that way. That is nonsense. If a tour is right for you and you enjoy yourself, who cares what anyone else thinks? Though I encourage independent travel, if it's not for you, then it's not. Don't let anyone make you feel like less of a traveler just because you're not sleeping under bridges.

That said, there are hundreds of tour companies competing for your travel dollar, and each has a different approach and level of service. The best way to choose among them is to contact two or three travel agents, get a bunch of brochures, and winnow them down to the best few prospects. Then talk to people who have taken those tours. If the company can't or won't provide you with names and numbers of satisfied customers, hold onto your wallet. The major complaint I hear concerns hidden costs on supposedly "all-inclusive" tours. Watch for these. Good luck, and remember to read the fine print.

If cars and the countryside go together like bacon and eggs, cars and cities go together like Twinkies and Tabasco. If you are interested mainly in rural areas and camping, think about a car. If you are going exclusively to major cities, the problems with parking, theft, and driving in traffic may not make it worth it. The expenses of renting a car can be horrific, especially if only paid by one person: $150–300 a week, depending on the country, for a car that moped riders will laugh at; add to this the cost of gas (roughly the cost of champagne in most European countries), a hefty tax, a collision damage waiver fee,

23

parking fees, road tolls, etc. All this makes renting only an affordable option for groups of two or more. Also, remember that every company has a minimum age for renters – either 21, 23, or 25.

One handy tip for those who do want to rent: It is almost always cheaper to arrange a rental vehicle before leaving instead of arranging it on the spot in Europe. It may also be cheaper to arrange a fly-drive package with a tour operator or travel agent. They will have much more buying clout than you as an individual, and even with their fees added on may be able to offer you substantial savings.

One friend, who is the king of the do-it-yourselfers, advocates buying a car, especially for motorhead types. If you are a good judge of cars and can bargain hard, you may be able to buy a car, use it, and sell it a few months later for almost as much as you paid for it. Don't bet the return ticket on this, and remember that you may end up driving around Paris looking for a shop that sells Armor-All so you can spiff the old sled up before you sell it. However, that's part of the experience, and even if you don't get quite as much as you paid for it, you will probably end up saving money over the rental option. You might, however, want to leave this for a second or later trip.

The indispensable guide to driving, buying, leasing and renting a car in Europe is *Moto Europa*, by Eric Bredesen (Seren Publishing, Dubuque, Iowa; ✆ 1-800-888-4741). I've never met Eric, but over the phone he certainly is very helpful and knowledgeable. He's hitching his way around the South Pacific by yacht at the moment, so he definitely qualifies as a hard-core budget traveler. He is also more enthusiastic about driving in Europe than I am. If you are seriously considering driving, buy his book. It will be $15.95 well spent.

Bicycles

If you haven't done a bike tour or two at home, I would strongly recommend against doing your first on your first trip to Europe. If you're going to pay the kind of money it takes to get across the ocean, you should make absolutely sure that you like pushing a bike around for six or eight hours a day.

Bike touring is one instance where an organized group trip, at least for first-timers, might make sense. Certainly the support that a company can provide, such as vans and repair facilities, can let the rider concentrate on biking rather than logistics. The classified section of any bicycling magazine (such as *Bicycling*) will have a number of ads for European trip outfitters. One warning, though: As with all types of tours, seemingly similar operations can have dramatically different levels of competence and professionalism. The best information you can possibly get on a company is a firsthand report from a rider who has recently taken a tour. A notice posted in a bike shop requesting firsthand accounts of European trips will probably get you more good advice than you can use.

Another option you might want to consider is a train/bike trip. Bikes are welcome on trains throughout Europe for a varying but usually small charge. By combining the two, you will be able to cover much more ground than by bike alone. Remember that the train system in Europe goes nearly everywhere; if you get sick of riding or of headwinds, the nearest train station will often be only a few kilometers away. On your return you can astound your friends with the number of countries you covered. Some tips for the prospective biker:

❖ Normally, you can bring your bike on an airplane as one of your two pieces of checked luggage for no charge (Delta, Virgin Atlantic, United, American, and others have this policy, but call to confirm for your airline and flight). Call your airline of choice for further details on packing, but expect them to insist that the bike is packed in some sort of protective, durable packaging – most airlines will sell you a standard-sized box for about ten bucks – and that the handlebars are turned sideways and the pedals and any baskets or panniers are taken off. You will probably need to check in an extra half-an-hour early.

❖ If you intend to rent a bike in Europe for a long ride, you might want to bring along a seat or a soft seat cover that you find comfortable. Rent a bike seats tend to be made from cast iron, or at least feel like it. Bringing your own helmet is also a good idea. I would never trust the safety of my skull to a rental helmet, or to no helmet at all. Bring one you have used before.

❖ Hopefully your bike weighs less than seventy pounds. If it does, you can pack other things in the box with it, both to avoid having to carry them with you and to pad the bike. Pad your faithful steed well, as fixing a damaged bike is a rotten way to start a trip.

❖ If you are a super-serious biker, remember that a trip to Europe is not a race, calling for an ultra-light, stripped-down speed machine. Hard as it may be, put a bell or a horn on your handlebars, as well as a big, un-aerody-namic (but safe) mirror. Lights can also be a lifesaver when you don't make your destination by nightfall. Along with tools, spare parts, and a good solid lock, bring extra sunscreen and lip balm.

❖ I strongly recommend getting around major cities by public transport instead of by bicycle. Remember that local drivers and local cyclists know what to expect from each other. The instinctive reactions that serve you so well at home may be just the wrong thing to do in Europe.

Despite much searching, I have yet to find a good book about bike touring in Europe. The two I have found, *Cycling Europe: Budget Bike Touring in the Old World*, by Nadine Slavinski (Bicycle Books), and *Europe by Bike*, Karen and Terry Whitehill (Mountaineers Press), are similar. They both have very short planning and basic information sections, and then present a number of routes and itineraries throughout Europe. Look before you buy.

If you are considering renting a bike while in Europe for a day or weekend, rather than as a primary means of getting around, see the section on bikes in Chapter 7.

Walking

If you are a dedicated walker, you are in for a treat. There are tens of thousands of miles of recognized trails in Europe, especially in the main mountain ranges of the Alps and Pyrenees, and in Great Britain and Ireland. In the United States and Canada, long-distance walking usually means hiking through the wilderness and camping. In Europe, on other hand, it can simply mean walking on a trail from cabin to cabin, or hostel to hostel, without the need for tent, groundsheet, sleeping pad, stove, and so on. In England you can easily hike from pub to pub over some truly beautiful farmland and end up gaining weight after walking eight hours a day. I'm sorry to say I've managed to do just that.

If you plan to do a walking trip, the first step is to write or call the tourist information offices mentioned earlier and request specific information on walking and hiking trails. Don't be surprised if you get more information than you can handle, particularly from Switzerland. Good maps are absolutely essential if you plan this sort of trip. You aren't going to be hiking in Alaska, but getting lost on the moors of England or in the mountains of France, Switzerland, or Italy, can be dangerous, especially considering the weather. Excellent maps, some designed specifically for the walker, are available in every country in Western Europe. If the local tourist office can't supply you with them, they can send you to someone who can. Invest in some even if you only plan a short hike.

WARNING: If you are planning on hiking in the woods of Eastern or Central Europe, see the health warning on tick encephalitis in Chapter 10.

CHAPTER THREE

BUDGETING

Budgeting is a touchy subject. Some people are going to have more money and/or different standards than others, some people are going to get lucky and find a great deal, while others may not. Also, everyone has an optimum point where they feel the trade-off between saving money and spending money is going to result in the best trip. On one hand, you really do want to save money, but on the other, you have spent quite a bit just to get to Europe, may not be back for years, and want to get as much out of the trip as possible. If you have a fixed amount of money, and I mean really fixed, the task is easier – you have to stick to that budget no matter what. For everyone else, that "rock-solid" budget may prove alarmingly expandable.

The brutal truth is that most of Europe is expensive. I took a seven-week trip to Europe specifically to prepare for writing this book, and saved every receipt, logged every expense, and tried to note every pound, mark, krone or franc I spent. It was an eye-opener. The minor expenses – tram tickets, tube tickets, museums, phone calls, ice cream, newspapers and so on – really do add up. Don't be surprised if you go over even the most carefully planned budget. Aussies and Kiwis should add about

US$300 to the budgets that follow to account for the higher airfares, while Brits can pretty much deduct the airfares altogether.

A Realistic Budget

The following is a budget for a typical two-month trip to Europe, for someone moving around quite a bit and seeing the sights. As you can see, it comes to about $3800, which is a realistic number to start with, with some of the inevitable budget bloat included. Note that the daily total, without transportation, is just over $40. You could certainly do it cheaper than this if you tried, but when I say realistic, I mean that this is a good framework to start planning from. I don't want to give too low a figure, and even this budget will take some disci-

pline. Increase all of these budgets by about $15 for every day you plan to spend in Denmark, Norway, Sweden, Finland, and Iceland.

Airline tickets	$650
15-day Eurail Youth Flexipass	$650
Accommodation (60 nights at $20 each)	$1200
Food/Alcohol (60 days at $12 each)	$720
Getting around in cities (50 days at $4 each)	$200
Documents (passport, student card, hostel card)	$100
Museum and Attraction admissions	$200
Incidentals	$100
Grand Total	**US $3820**

Middle to Low-Range Budgets

Going cheaper than the above is certainly possible. Airline tickets should be somewhat cheaper from the East Coast, or a great deal or sale could cut their price. Don't plan on this, though; prices could just as easily go up. Camping would help the most and could cut that $1200 chunk by half. It would do this, however, at an increased cost in city transportation, and greatly increased time spent toting packs around. A cheaper train pass or a bus pass could help squeeze a bit, as could cheaper food and fewer incidentals – buying food at stores and cooking it for yourself can save major dollars. If you like pasta, or rather if you like cooking pasta, you can eat cheaply pretty much everywhere. Traveling as a couple, you can save some money over single travelers, and you will have more privacy while you save.

Unless you want to hitchhike, sleep in train stations, and eat bread three meals a day, I would count on spending an absolute minimum of about $3000 for two months. This is a daily total of about $31 per day, without transportation. Note that this last budget cannot be cut substantially anywhere.

Airline tickets	$650
10-day Eurail Youth Flexipass	$470
Food (60 days at $10 each)	$600
Accommodation (50 nights at $6, 10 nights at $20)	$500
Getting around in cities (50 days at $7 each)	$350
Documents (passport, student card, hostel card)	$100
Museum and Attraction admissions	$200
Incidentals	$100
Grand Total	**US $2970**

Rock-Bottom Budgets

If you are reading this and it seems that Europe is beyond your reach, take heart. A two-month trip with train pass is not mandatory. Below I have set out a one-month ultra-budget trip. This trip will require some major creativity on your part, like arranging transportation between where you want to go. And at four dollars a day for city transportation, you will be walking a lot in the cities. You shouldn't hitchhike unless you are very comfortable with the idea, but you may be able to appeal to other hostelers who have a vehicle. Keep your ears wide open. I sincerely doubt if you could do better than this – certainly don't count on it.

Airline tickets	$650
Accommodation (10 nights at $20, 20 nights at $6)	$320
Food (30 days at $10 each)	$300
Getting around in cities (30 days at $4 each)	$120
Documents (passport, student card, hostel card)	$100
Museum and Attraction admissions	$100
Incidentals	$100
Grand Total	**US $1690**

If you think you can do it cheaper...

I'm sure there's some go-cheap commando out there who claims to have been traveling since 1967 on less than the $1700 I mention. If you have done that, or know how to live on less than, say, $25 a day while seeing something of Europe, I'd love to hear from you. I cannot in good conscience advise a lower budget for the first-timer, unless you have extensive cheap travel experience in the States or your home country; or you have contacts in Europe who would be willing to put you up when you arrive penniless at their door. Do not try the "I can get *there* – I'll worry about getting *back* later" approach. And don't even think about the idea of "I can always appeal to the embassy – they won't abandon a fellow citizen so far from home." They will. Your nation's embassies overseas will barely notice if you drop dead in their doorways. Providing irresponsible travelers with money to get home is not their top priority, and believe me, they have heard every sob story known to man.

Don't Overeconomize!

Those are the numbers. They may not be exact, but they do represent a realistic estimate of what a trip to Europe will cost. Remember that some of the expenses listed, such as food, would also have to be paid for if you stayed home. If you consider that you may not be paying rent while you travel, nor driving your car if you have one, the cost picture may look a lot better. Subletting or moving out of your apartment can obviously save a great deal of money and can mean the difference between going and staying for many people, especially students. I recommend subletting, but this is difficult in most university towns, so try to arrange it as early as possible.

At the risk of driving you into debt, here's my philosophy on spending on a European trip. If this is going to be the trip of a lifetime, spend a bit more and have the kind of trip you want. Students, trust me, $300 buys a lot more happiness at twenty than at thirty, even if you could afford to take the whole summer off to go travel at that age. Since many students are graduating with a pretty hefty debt anyway, a few hundred bucks on top of that pile is not going to seem like much, especially when viewed from the distance of a couple of years. For both students and nonstudents, if you have the money, there are few better places to spend it than in Florence, Dublin, Barcelona, or Prague.

●●

EXTRA MONEY, YOU SAY?

Not everyone is on the strictest of budgets. For those fortunate few of you who are not, realize that your extra money can go pretty far in Europe. If I had, say, one thousand dollars to add to my "realistic budget," my first priority would be to buy more rail travel power. As I detail in *Basics* #2, an unlimited pass is more than worth the money it costs. The next upgrade would be for accommodations – an occasional hotel to break up the hostel routine. After that would come food, then some truly nice souvenirs. Last on the list would be getting around in cities and upgraded air travel. I'm not mentioning museums because, as I will discuss in a few pages, museums, monuments, and other cultural attractions should never be scrimped on in the first place.

••

Working Abroad

Here's a hot tip: There is one country where working to earn money for a European trip is better than any other. There are no language problems, no problems with taxes or laws, and the wages are relatively high. On top of that, prospective European travelers are welcomed wholeheartedly by the locals. This wondrous country, for Americans, is called the United States of America. Another profound truth learned at great pain. The best place for Americans to work to pay for a European trip is right at home. Why go to Europe and get some miserable low-paying job that barely covers food and rent when you could sacrifice some free time in the States and then travel without the need to work? Oh, yeah: "But I'll be in Europe while I work." True, but you will be working, possibly illegally, probably very hard, and probably for low wages, and all the while your vacation will be ticking by. Why not sacrifice some time at home and earn the money here, with housing, transportation, and all the other life issues already settled? Just my opinion. If you have a great job lined up in Europe, that's different. If the money earned is secondary to the purpose of being immersed more deeply in the culture, by all means, go for that job. But to earn money efficiently, there's no place like home.

For Canadians, Kiwis, Aussies, and those from other Commonwealth countries, the picture is slightly different. Britain has a policy of allowing descendants of its former colonists back to the motherland to work, though with restrictions. Commonwealth citizens with one or more grandparent born in Britain do not need a work permit at all, though they must apply for entry. Commonwealth citizens between ages 17 and 26 can apply to be "working holiday-makers" and stay for up to two years, though working no more than half the time of their stay.

As far as working in the rest of the European Union, every country has different rules, and none are exactly screaming for hordes of travelers to come and take high-paying jobs. Brits have full EU privileges, of course, and Commonwealth citizens mentioned above may be able to use their British entry as a Trojan Horse to work in other nations. Also, if you have a parent or grandparent who emigrated from a European country, contact its embassy to see if you have similar privileges. Ireland and Greece, in particular, are supposed to welcome home prodigal descendants. Regardless of your status, if you wish to work in a particular country, contact that embassy months before leaving to get all details and necessary forms, so you can lineup something well in advance. Even then, expect a few snags before it's over. Good luck.

WARNING: Any readers planning on working in Britain without permission, or entering Europe via Britain with the intention of working in another country, should see the section on British immigration officials in Chapter 12.

Shorter Trips

If you are working, rather than a student, teacher, or person of independent wealth, spending a whole summer wandering around Europe is probably not possible. For someone who has only two or three weeks to travel, the priorities change. Planning ahead to make the most of your limited time is essential, and a trip can and should be planned out day by day. Not very spontaneous, I know, but two weeks just doesn't allow for that. On the other hand, two weeks is plenty of time to see some truly wonderful places in Europe, and is a heck of a lot better than not going at all. Also, the short-term traveler has one huge advantage over the summer traveler: the ability to go before June or after August. If you have a choice, by all means avoid the summer crowds and heat and go in spring or early fall. Between October and April, however, you should expect some fairly cold weather, even in southern Europe. Some thoughts about a two- or three-week trip:

❖ Decide whether you want to explore one or two cities or see the most famous bits of three or four. Anything more than four cities (or two regions) is going to be too much.

❖ Traveling by night train is highly recommended, especially if you are able to get a decent night's sleep in a somewhat noisy environment. More on this in the section on trains.

❖ Carefully check the operating days and hours for any museums or attractions you especially want to see, and plan accordingly. These should be listed in your guidebook. Many museums in Europe are closed on Mondays, so you might want to plan on traveling then. There are exceptions to this rule; the Louvre, for example, is closed on Tuesdays, but open late on Mondays and Wednesdays. National tourist offices should also be able to tell in advance if any major attractions are likely to be closed or under renovation. Be careful – a lot of renovation is going on these days.

❖ A full Eurail pass will not be necessary, and any train pass may prove too expensive unless you are really moving around. Do not buy a pass unless you are sure you will need it. Most travel agencies that sell Eurail passes also quote prices for individual train tickets. Compare the price of separate train or bus tickets with the cheapest possible pass (see *Basics* #2) that will cover your trip.

❖ Look very hard for an airfare that allows you to leave from the last city you plan to see, rather than one that requires you to fly out of the city you flew into. It is well worth paying a hundred dollars or more for this option, although it may not be necessary to pay anything extra at all.

❖ One good thing about going for two weeks is that it gives you the option of taking a courier flight, delivering documents or a package to a European city, which may work out even cheaper than discounted tickets. See the section on couriers and charters in Chapter 5.

❖ When all of the planning and expense is considered, a three-week trip is much more than a 50 percent improvement over a two-week trip. If you can borrow a week from next year's vacation time, consider it. Also, if you can afford it, see if you can get another week off unpaid.

You really can see quite a bit in two weeks. If I were going for that length of time – and bear in mind that I like art, architecture and that kind of stuff – I would probably advise something like this:

Day 1:	Fly to London.
Days 2–5:	London, and perhaps Cambridge or Oxford.
Days 6–9:	Channel Tunnel train to Paris. Paris, Chartres, and Versailles. Night train to Rome.
Days 10–13:	Rome, with a day trip to Florence.
Day 14:	Fly home out of Rome.
Day 15:	Fight jet lag, and drive your friends insane with jealousy by casually referring to "Firenze" and "Roma."

If you have three weeks, I would recommend adding one day in or around London, two days in Paris, one day in Florence, two days in Venice, and a day trip from Rome to Naples/Pompeii.

Veteran travelers may sneer at such a "short" trip, but who cares? In those two weeks you can see, roughly in order, Westminster Abbey, Big Ben, the Houses of Parliament, Trafalgar Square, the Tower of London and the Crown Jewels, Piccadilly Circus, Buckingham Palace, the British Museum and National Gallery, Cambridge University, the Eiffel Tower, Notre Dame, Versailles, the Mona Lisa, the Louvre, the Cathedral at Chartres, the Sistine Chapel, Vatican City, the Spanish Steps, the Trevi Fountain, the Colosseum, the Uffizi Gallery, and Michelangelo's *David*. Or you could blow off this itinerary entirely and spend two weeks whooping it up in Paris, Cannes, Milan, or Mallorca. Or, like one person I know, you could spend two weeks in Belgium and the

Netherlands, ignore everything on the above itinerary, and still feel as if there was much more to see in those two small countries.

So you're hitting the tourist highlights and not spending a month hanging out in Parisian cafés drinking cheap wine and talking about Camus and Sartre with a bunch of long-haired pseudointellectuals. So what? You've been to Europe once, and if you like it, you can always go back and see more, with all the experience gained on your first trip. And until that next trip you've still got Vienna, Munich, Berlin, and a dozen other incredible places to look forward to. Sounds all right to me.

• •

OLDER TRAVELERS

Older travelers shouldn't be deterred from touring Europe independently or on a budget – believe me, there are plenty of other people your age doing it. "Youth Hostels" have renamed and reinvented themselves as places where anyone can stay, regardless of age (except in Bavaria, which clings to a limit of 26 and under). There are even "elder hostels" if you can't stomach the idea of youth hostels. Make inquiries of tourist offices if you are interested in these, both before you go and while you're abroad. The only real age penalty I can think of is with some train passes and tickets, which must be validated before the user's 26th birthday. However, there are passes specifically designed for seniors. And if you are fifty or older, bring proof of that fact. There are hundreds of discounts in Europe for seniors as well as for the young. Other than that, I've just made a few special notes throughout the text that relate specifically to older travelers, and remember, I've managed to fill an entire book with advice for travelers of all ages.

• •

Saving Money

While in Europe you will obviously want to spend wisely, and not spend money unnecessarily. The most flexible budget items are museums and attractions, and food and drink, and the amount spent on either is entirely a matter of personal preference. My thoughts on these follow; as always, take them for what they're worth in your situation and on your trip.

Museums

Don't try to go cheap here. By all means, skip a museum because you're sick of them and don't want to see another painting for the rest of your life, but don't skip a major museum just to save money. For example, there is a copy of Michelangelo's *David* in the main square of Florence. Since there is usually a line and always a charge (about $7 without a discount) to see the real thing, some people are satisfied to see the copy. I agree that $7 is a lot of money to pay to see one statue, but when you get home you will probably regret not seeing the real, honest-to-God *David* for about the price of a movie. (You should regret it, by the way. The copy is *nothing* like the real thing.) If you are going to a large number of museums, however, this can cost some serious money: Five dollars here and four dollars there can add up. Some hints:

◆ Going to Europe without an International Student Identification Card (ISIC) or a youth or teacher card if you are eligible, or not using one if you have one, is simply throwing money away. See Chapter 4 for more on these.

◆ Many cities sell "Tourist Cards," or "City Passports," good for admission to large numbers of museums or attractions. As a bonus, a few also offer head-of-the-line privileges. That's worth a lot on a hot summer day, believe you me. Check and see if a particular card allows unlimited entries for a certain time period, or only one per card. Then check and see how the cost stacks up against the cost of what you really want to see. If it's close, buy one, and you may end up going to more exhibits than planned, with some pleasant surprises. The existence of these cards is usually detailed in your guidebooks. Always check for them before arrival, or at the tourist office when you get there.

❖ Many museums have a reduced- or free-admissions day some time during the week or month. If this day is during the week, it can be worth waiting for. If it's on a Sunday, expect major crowds. If you want to visit a museum briefly, or for a second time, remember that some – the Louvre in Paris, for example – have reduced admission prices in the afternoon. Remember, many European museums are closed on Mondays.

❖ Whether or not to pay to see the *David* is, at least in my opinion, an easy decision. Other museums housing less impressive or famous exhibits are not quite so easy. Again it's a judgment call, balancing money, interest, time, and tiredness, for you to make. Be wary of some smaller private museums, though. Many are little more than thinly disguised gift shops. The real finds are usually the obscure public museums, where you may be one of the only visitors. I have seldom regretted paying for a museum and have often found really marvelous things in small, out-of-the-way exhibits. Be warned, though: I sometimes regret not spending the seven bucks to get into the Liberace museum in Las Vegas, so I may have a different standard than you . . .

Food and Drink

Food and drink, especially if you drink alcohol, are probably the all-time European budget-busting champions, with food taking overall honors by a nose. Whenever possible, buy food in stores, head for the nearest park, and chow down. This can lead to a somewhat dull diet of bread, yogurt, cheese, and fruit (the four basic European traveler's foods), but you won't spend much money and you will eat fairly well. Europeans (the English and Scandinavians are notable exceptions) may have a different idea of what breakfast means than Americans and Canadians do – typically some form of bread and coffee – so be sure to ask what you are going to get before buying that hostel breakfast. In Scandinavia, hostel breakfasts are typically fairly elaborate affairs of yogurt, muesli, fish and so on, and are usually very good deals. Whenever you have a chance to all-you-can-eat in Scandinavia, you should – and eat until you are bloated like a beached whale. Food is very expensive in those countries. In England, the cholesterol assault known as the full English breakfast can keep you going until dinner if you adopt the same tactic of scarfing until you can barely walk.

Eating out can be one of the really charming aspects of European travel. Remember, though, "authentic" and "local" do not always mean "expensive." Good, cheap restaurants can be few and far between, especially in cities, but they do exist: the best sources of information on such places are your hostel or pension staff, your fellow travelers, and your guidebook, usually in that order. The usual list of thoughts and experiences:

✧ Any restaurant that caters excessively to tourists should be avoided, just as you would avoid the same type of place at home. Menus in English are usually a bad sign.

✧ Some of the things that come free in Canada, the States, or other countries, such as bread, butter, and so on, sometimes cost extra in Europe. If something magically appears on your table that you did not order, you should inquire about its price.

✧ You can often eat at bars as well, but you should know that in continental Europe prices for the same item in a bar or café can increase dramatically when you sit at a table, instead of standing at a table or at the counter, if any. This is less true the farther north you go, culminating with the traditional English pub or Dutch "brown café," where you can sit anywhere you like.

• •

THE McDONALD'S FACTOR

You will go to and eat at a McDonald's when you are in Europe. Yes, I know that you wouldn't be caught dead in one while in the States, and, yes, if you took a date to one in your hometown, you would face a hurricane of ridicule and abuse. Yes, I know that you are going to Europe to experience authentic foreign culture, not transplanted American fast food. However, you will go to and eat at a McDonald's while you are in Europe. Why? The bathrooms will be the initial lure. Clean, free, convenient bathrooms with guaranteed toilet paper can be few and far between in some cities (Paris springs to mind instantly). When you have once crossed the threshold, half the battle is over, and you are all but lost. The familiarity starts to work: "Hey, this is just like back home. . ." "Smells pretty good, and I can get something familiar, in a hurry, and it's not too expensive. . . "Well, maybe just this once. . ." And the next thing you know you're chowing down a double bacon McBurger, large fries please, and a medium Coke. Resistance is futile. Though you have been warned, it will help you not. The Golden Arches will triumph in the end.

• •

Alcohol

Alcohol, while often expensive, is certainly a big part of going out in Europe. I think it was Woody Allen that was thrown out of a restaurant in France for not ordering wine with a meal. German and British beers, French and Italian wines, Spanish sherries and Portuguese ports, Scotch and Irish whiskies, anisette, grappa, ouzo – the list goes on. Some of it great, some of it interesting, some of it (Italian Cynar, Scandinavian aquavit) just plain vile. And depending on the country, it can be either dirt cheap or incredibly expensive. In Scandinavia, as detailed below, the price is so high that it has made alcohol consumption something of a mania. In other places, especially Eastern Europe (beer) and France and Italy (wine), alcohol may be cheaper than soft drinks or even bottled water, especially if you buy it from a supermarket.

When in Europe, it's worth spending a bit more and trying a better version of the local product as opposed to brands sold internationally – or even in other parts of the country. Whatever it is may take some getting used to, but that's part of the experience. On the downside, be aware that drunk tourists are a criminal's dream – if you're going out to get hammered, go in a group. Note also that the legal limits for blood alcohol while driving in most, if not all, European countries are very low. More than one beer will put you over the limit in Sweden. The penalties for drunk driving are savage, too; if I remember right, a 0.08 blood alcohol content (three or four beers) results in a mandatory two- or three-week jail sentence in Norway. The designated driver was an established institution among European teens twenty or thirty years ago. If you and your friends are driving to a night out, use one.

● ●

A RIDE ON A SCANDINAVIAN FERRY

One of the more bizarre experiences you can have in Europe is an overnight ride on an international Scandinavian ferry. "Ferry" doesn't do these vessels justice: A modern version of this type of ship is more like a combination floating hotel, shopping mall and entertainment district. Because of stiff value-added and other taxes (see the following section), alcohol costs a fortune in Scandinavian countries. Scandinavians have gotten around this by moving their liquor stores onto boats, and then floating those boats out to international waters, where the taxes don't apply. Transportation is almost secondary to the real mission of these ships, which is to allow the passengers to avoid taxes and have a rollicking good time while doing so. The result is astonishing. Massive, glittering ferries, some with glass elevators on the entry deck, many holding thousands of people, and all with enormous stores full of foreign-made cigarettes, candy, consumer goods, and incredible amounts of every conceivable form of booze. Along with the stores there are restaurants, discos, bars, lounges, and so on. Picture a floating casino where the emphasis is on buying and boozing instead of gambling. After the territorial limit is cleared the stores are the scene of a buying frenzy that defies belief. Then some of the products bought are hurriedly consumed on the spot, with the end result being a boat full of well-fed, partying drunks. It's like a scene from the day Prohibition was repealed.

● ●

Value-Added Tax

Many European countries are expensive in part because of value-added tax, which is like a super-hefty sales tax and averages about 17 percent. If you are buying something expensive and leaving the country afterward, you can often get some of this tax refunded (in fact, many countries require a fairly healthy minimum purchase before you qualify for the refund). If you make a major purchase, this can save big bucks, and can also make something that you couldn't afford without the refund fit into your budget. The procedures for doing this are usually complicated, and should be explained by a tourist office or at a more upscale store. Look for the blue-and-red or blue-and-silver signs that say "Tax Free for Tourists" – these places can give you a check for the amount of tax you have paid on the spot, and this can usually be cashed at the airport or sent in after you get home. If you wait until you get home, don't count on getting your refund right away.

CHAPTER FOUR

WHAT TO TAKE

The best advice I can give on this subject, and the second of the Three Great Travel Commandments, is the following: *Travel Light*. I know you've heard it before, but I doubt you believe it. Consider this: *Every* first-time traveler I have asked has said that they wished they hadn't brought so much with them. Every one. Please, please, please, believe me. I have met Australians who have been traveling for six months with a daypack. I once made a two-week side trip from London to Cadiz, Spain, via Madrid, Paris, and Granada, also with a daypack. It was great. I truly believe that the most important thing you can do to ensure an enjoyable trip is to bring only what's genuinely necessary with you. Clothes are the worst culprit – bringing too many will make you feel that you spent two months doing nothing but carrying a giant mass of dirty laundry around Europe. I can think of one idiot who brought so many clothes on his first trip that he had to pay an excess baggage fee. (I've learned my lesson since then.) You will be happiest if you bring no more than what you can carry on to the airplane: a large, well-made daypack or a small travel pack. If you can carry all that you've brought around a museum, you've done just about right on the weight.

I can practically hear the snorts of disbelief and derision as you read this: "Yeah right, pal, like I can really live two months out of a daypack." Well, no, actually you can live out of a daypack indefinitely. You honestly can. Someone once said: "Figure out exactly what you need for your trip, then bring twice the money and half the clothes." Words of wisdom. Some of the benefits of packing light:

❖ You don't have to check your bag when flying, and therefore never lose control of your things. While others may have their bags sent to Zambia, you are sitting pretty. This is no joke – having your bags lost is a miserable experience.

❖ You can spend more time, if you so choose, looking for accommodation, and don't have to fight that common, desperate desire to accept any place to stay just so you can take off your damn pack. Believe me, you'll appreciate this greatly when you're on the road.

❖ You aren't chained to a bag. After a week of travel with too much stuff, that's how it feels, and it gets worse. For example: You have a 1pm train. You would like to spend the morning in a museum or a park. With tons of stuff you either have to leave your things at your hotel or hostel, if possible, and return there before catching the train, or leave your things in a locker or at the left- luggage office in the train station, and then go back out. When you're light and mobile, you just put on your pack, go where you want to go, and only go to the station to catch your train.

❖ The mental strain is less. You'll understand it better once you're in Europe, but a big bag is just a major headache to worry about, almost like a traveling companion you hate. There is a definite feeling of release after you find a place to leave your stuff, roughly equivalent to being let out of school. If you have a really big bag, the feeling is like being let out of a cage.

● ●

CARRY-ON BAGGAGE

Airlines' maximum carry-on size varies, despite what some authors claim. Typically, length plus width plus height must be less than 45 inches, with some airlines allowing 55 inches. Weights allowed vary from eleven measly pounds on British Airways to a back-straining seventy pounds on American. Call your airline for details. In real life, you will rarely be challenged on your carry-on unless it's suitcase size, and most airlines will also allow two small pieces instead of just one.

● ●

ESSENTIALS

As I'm sure you're sick of hearing already, packing light is A Very Good Thing. On the other hand, there are many items that are essential and should be brought with you, and some others that are very handy but might not be immediately obvious. There is a checklist of stuff to take in *Basics #11*, but I'm also going to go through my recommendations of what to bring and what not to bring item by item. If you're buying things specifically for your trip, remember that quality is definitely cheapest in the long run. In particular, the six things you do not want to skimp on are your main pack, daypack, camera, shoes, guidebook, and map(s). Each of these is vital to your trip, and saving money by buying a cheap version of any of them is asking for trouble. The best book on selecting packs, shoes, and a number of other relevant items is *Backpacking One Step at a Time* by Harvey Manning (Vintage Books). Although this book is written primarily for campers, the sections on packs, boots, and equipment are more than worth the price. Manning has probably forgotten more about those three subjects than I ever knew.

Luggage

I almost called this section "backpacks" because the idea of suitcases seems so outlandish. Backpacks are hard enough to carry around. Suitcases, gym bags, duffle bags, *anything* designed to be carried by hand, including bags with one shoulder strap, have no place on any trip that involves using public transportation and walking. Any budget traveler will be doing both of these quite a bit. Luggage with wheels is made for airports, and will not last if used extensively on sidewalks or streets. Even if you will be using your own or a rental car, backpacks of one sort or another are the way to go. If you don't like the idea of backpacks, then buy a travel pack (see below) and use it as a suitcase; that way you will have the ability to switch carrying modes if you find that carrying your things by hand is too difficult. Leaving the suitcases home goes double for older travelers. Break the habits of a lifetime and invest in a travel pack. Trust me, you'll be glad you did.

No matter what you choose, buy something solid that will last a lifetime, especially since buying something new in Europe will bankrupt you. Also, attach a large, solid name tag with your name, a dollar or two, and the phone number of someone at home inside your bag. That way, if your bag is lost and found, the finder can call, at your cost, and let someone know where it is. After getting to Europe, a name tag, with phone number, on the outside is a good idea, especially if you lock your bag. Also, sewing a clip on the inside of your bag and clipping away any keys you might need on your return keeps them safe and out of the way.

Travel Packs

A travel pack is basically soft luggage, with a very simple internal frame, shoulder straps, a waist belt, and a flap that can be used to cover the straps and belt and convert the whole thing into a suitcase. A relatively new product, these packs are probably the best choice for most travelers, especially those not intending to do much hiking. They certainly are extremely popular, although they are marginal at best for long walks, and anything over a mile or so with one is going to be unpleasant, especially if the pack is fully loaded. For short walks, however, they are fine, and light years better than duffle bags or suitcases. A major plus of travel packs is that they usually have a zipper that allows the whole pack to be split open, thus avoiding lots of digging and groping around. Since travel packs are designed for travel rather than hiking, they can almost always be locked up – a very handy feature. Cost: $140–250.

Backpacks

Backpacks fall into two main categories: those with external frames and those with internal frames. Although external frames are often looked upon as obsolete or "low-class," they are still the best choice if you are going to be walking long distances with your pack on roads or trails. If you are planning on walking in Switzerland or trekking in Scotland, if walking is in any way the focus of your trip, this is the way to go. The disadvantages of an external frame are its rigidity, making it difficult to fit into lockers, the tendency for the frame, straps, and buckles to be damaged when checked on airplanes, and the typical lack of any way to lock the darn thing. If you are going to travel with an external frame, box it up before putting it on the plane to Europe. If you don't, the baggage system may destroy it, and you can watch the pieces come spilling out onto the carousel (along with chunks of your camera, shreds of your clothes, dirty underwear, and so on). For the return, if you can't find a box, tighten the straps up and then mummify it with a roll of plastic packing tape. A decent external frame pack will cost $120–220.

A good internal frame pack carries a load almost as well as an external frame and is somewhat less liable to damage. However, you should still tighten straps, and box or tape it if possible before entrusting it to an airline. Internal frames usually reflect a more modern design than external frames and have become the packs of choice for most hikers. This is not entirely a reflection of utility, however. The latest word on carrying a large load is that external frames are slightly better if you are on streets or trails, while internal frames, which more closely hug the body, are better for scrambling on rocks and across rough country. If that's the primary purpose of your trip, you probably have a backpack already. Completely locking an internal frame is usually not possible. Cost: $150–300.

Moutaineering Packs

These are essentially very large and sophisticated daypacks, with waist belts, designed for mountaineers or rock climbers. A medium-sized one is about the right size, and can be carried on an airplane, thereby eliminating the risk of damage by belligerent baggage handlers. They're difficult to lock, though, and sometimes a bit too long and narrow when you need to pull something from the bottom of the pack. Cost: $80–160.

Daypacks

A good daypack should be your constant companion, containing your camera, film, notebook, guidebook, maps and all those bits and pieces you need every day. If you follow my advice, you'll get a big one and live out of it. If not, then go for a medium-sized, high-quality lockable version. Spend some time finding one that you like, since you will be using it a lot. I also recommend getting one with a zipper that goes around the perimeter of the pack, so you can open it up completely. This prevents groping, or having to pour out all of the contents to find a small item. By the way, fanny packs are no substitute for a daypack; they are too small, and are much more vulnerable to theft.

Some travel packs have daypacks that zip onto the larger pack. While this seems like a neat idea, it puts your most important and valuable things hanging out there in the breeze, out of your sight and out of your feeling, and practically in the hands of razor-wielding thieves. A terrible idea. It is far better to leave enough space to fit your daypack inside your main pack, where it will be out of sight, and leave you only one piece to worry about. If this is too heavy, or you don't have space, wear your daypack in front of you, as you will see most experienced travelers doing. This will also help balance the weight of your main pack when you walk.

Backpack Essentials

Nothing beats experience. Before buying a new backpack, borrow one of the same type from a friend, get their thoughts on it, load it up with clothes and books, and take it for a walk around the neighborhood. I guess if you truly want to be realistic, walk from house to house, up and down stairs in blazing sun, to simulate a search for accommodation in Rome. Also, most backpacking shops, especially the small ones, will have experienced employees that will give the shopper tons of advice. Once you settle on the type you want you can start shopping around (see *Basics* #7 for a list of suppliers). Don't wait until the last minute to buy your pack – order or buy it at least a month before you go. When you get it, as before, load it up with stuff and take it for a good long walk at least once. If you can't get comfortable with it, or you find some problem and have to return it, that's the time to find out, not the day you intend to leave. By the way, if you take about ten of those walks, you will not only know your backpack better, but also have a much better idea of how much your pack really weighs (taking that leather trench coat to Europe may not seem worth it after all), you will have spent lots of time out in the healthy fresh air and sunshine, and your feet will not rise in savage protest when you start your march across Europe. I have to admit that I haven't always prepared like this. You can read about the gruesome consequences later.

How you pack a backpack is almost as important to your comfort as how much goes in it. Ideally, you want the smallest possible pack that conforms to your body shape as much as possible. This will keep the weight on the waist belt and off your shoulders and will greatly increase the ease of carrying your pack. Almost all modern packs have external straps to tighten the whole thing up after packing. If you've got them, use them, and get your pack as tight and compact as you can.

When carrying a load, at least 50 percent of the work should be done by the waist belt. Your belt should be as tight as is comfortable, and you should be able to slide a finger or a hand through the front of your shoulder straps when standing straight up. The whole aim of good packing is to get as much weight as possible bearing vertically on your hips and legs, and as little as possible pulling back and down on your relatively weaker shoulders. If your pack does not have a waist belt, don't take it to Europe unless it's the size of a daypack. Trust me on this one.

Finally, it's a good idea to take a large waterproof bag to cover your backpack in case of rain. If you expect rain on your trip, get a solid one made of plastic, vinyl, or waterproof cloth. If you are pretty sure of good weather, two or three thick hefty bags somewhere in your pack will serve.

Backpack Locks

Most travel packs can and should be locked with a small padlock. It's best not to buy the tiny locks you see advertised in travel equipment catalogs; you can get the same thing for about one-fifth the price at a hardware store. Either way, these locks won't stop someone who's determined, but they will discourage the casual or opportunistic thief.

Clothes

I've said it before and I may as well say it again here – keep your clothes to an absolute minimum. This is where most people lose the battle against excess weight.

Remember also that all of your clothes are going to get some hard use. One school of thought says that because of this, you should bring old stuff; another says that because of this, new things would be better. I prefer to bring new things; after a few weeks on the road I look scroungy enough without old or worn clothes adding to the effect. Also, remember that you can always buy clothes on the road if you need them.

For both men and women, the list should look something like the following:

◆ One pair (possibly two) of long pants, preferably not faded blue jeans if you intend to do some stepping out. Also, long pants or skirts are required in some churches, most notably St. Peter's in Rome. New black Levis have served me well but are a bit hot in the summer. I usually buy something lighter when the weather gets hot and shorts are inappropriate. One belt as well.
◆ One nice short-sleeve shirt with a collar.
◆ Two T-shirts, preferably non-white and in good shape.
◆ One long-sleeve oxford-type shirt, definitely not white, or a similar shirt for women. Women might also want to include one more long-sleeved top for use in countries where bare female skin is frowned upon in public.
◆ One hooded sweatshirt or a rugby shirt, long- or short-sleeved. A nice-looking dark sweater can also serve many of the same functions, and can also be worn on a more dressy occasion. Sweatshirts with college names look touristy, but can be good for trading with European students.
◆ Two pairs of shorts, again nonwhite.
◆ Five sets of underwear. Add a set of long underwear if you are going somewhere cold.
◆ Six or seven pairs of socks. If you're going to a cold area, make two pairs of these wool. Seven may seem like a lot, but you will definitely lose some, and they weigh very little.
◆ One pair of no-kidding, fully functional walking shoes. See the following page for more on this.
◆ A pair of solid walking sandals (rather than a pair of cheap thongs), for slimy showers, the beach, or kicking back.
◆ Your rain gear. Again, see the next page for more.

❖ A hat with a brim. If you're going into the mountains or to a cold area, a wool watch cap also.

❖ A bandanna or two. The red kind, usually seen around the necks of golden retrievers, has 1001 uses. Women should also include some form of head covering to wear in churches and in some of the smaller Mediterranean villages.

❖ A bathing suit, preferably one that can be used as extra underwear or shorts.

❖ A skirt for women, preferably long, loose, light, and opaque. Not too long, though, as you will probably be climbing stairs in it.

❖ A coat in some form, preferably loose enough to layer over other things. If this can also serve as your raincoat (see below), so much the better.

Shoes

A blister the size of a pencil eraser can make you absolutely miserable on vacation. Larger ones can make you wish you'd stayed home. Wearing a pair of cheap, too-old, too-new, or poorly fitting shoes to Europe is a recipe for a horrendous trip. You will be walking a long way no matter how you travel, so come prepared. Whatever you choose to wear – Birkenstocks, Air Jordans, stiletto heels, whatever – make sure that they will last at least another few months and are properly broken in. Take at least one five-mile walk in them and see how they feel at the end of it. Put new laces on them before you go. Yes, I know it's obvious, but it still bears repeating. The largest blister I've ever seen (the size and shape of half a golf ball) was on an American traveler in Munich who came to Europe wearing a brand new pair of shoes.

Rain Gear

Gore-Tex rules here, if you can afford the stuff. My favorite traveling companion is a 'tex jacket that has a separate liner that can be zipped in or out, depending on the temperature. Get a jacket with a removable hood if you can. Unless you are going to be spending most of your time in England, Ireland, Scotland, or Scandinavia, or planning on some serious hiking elsewhere, you probably won't need a full-length raincoat or Gore-Tex pants. For serious trekkers, a knee-length waterproof coat with a hood is advisable. For all travelers, a small, high-quality umbrella is very handy to have in one's daypack, especially in the countries just mentioned.

Other Essentials

There are any number of other things you should probably have with you, and to save your having to rack your brains for them all, I've included a list of the most likely items here.

A Money Belt or Neck Wallet

This kind of thing is as mandatory a piece of gear as I can think of. The security section (Chapter 12) details why. Actually, "money belt" is a bit of a misnomer; they're really small, flat pouches large enough to hold a passport, money, and other necessary documents, with elastic belts attached. Neck wallets are a bit smaller, hang on a line around the neck, and are more suited for emergency supplies of cash or credit cards, as they can't hold much else. The money belts made by Eagle Creek are industry standard; they are available from the suppliers listed in *Basics #7*.

A Padlock and Chain or Cable

This combination is essential, especially for solo travelers. The lock is needed for lockers in hostels, and with the cable, can be used to secure your pack to train luggage racks, another pack, etc. Those old reliable Master combination padlocks from junior high are perfect. Avoid keys for obvious reasons. For the cable, try to get something at least 48 inches long and a quarter-inch thick, or the same length of solid chain. The cables sold at bike shops that are curled up like a slinky and coated with plastic are perfect. If your hostel or pension doesn't have any lockers, chaining your pack to a bed, pipe, or other solid object, by the shoulder straps, is a good idea. Obviously, a determined thief could cut the straps, but that would leave him with a ruined, awkward-to-carry backpack. Really, you're just trying to deter the opportunistic thief, or at least make him pick somebody else's bag.

A First-Aid Kit

I'm always surprised at how much I use my first-aid kit, and how useful it proves to other people. If nothing else, it will save you the time and expense of buying a whole box of Band Aids when you only need one. Above all, you should realize that it is far cheaper and better to assemble your own kit than to pay big bucks for the false security that most prepackaged kits on the market provide. Mine includes a bunch of Band-Aids, including some large square ones for scrapes, a roll of gauze, twenty iodine wipes, a tube of antiseptic ointment, a roll of athletic tape, moleskin for blister relief, five needles and a lighter to sterilize them, twenty aspirin, a pair of tweezers, and an airline bottle of Scotch for use on sore throats. It weighs about eight ounces. A more elaborate kit is essential for hikers.

Bug Repellent

If you're visiting Scotland (midges) or the countryside in Holland or Scandinavia (saber-toothed mosquitoes), you absolutely must have some sort of bug repellent; and it's handy to have when camping out anywhere. When buying this stuff, check the label for the amount of active ingredients; anything under about 25 percent will be ineffective. Creams and liquids such as *Cutter* or *Jungle Juice* are better than sprays. Be very careful with some of the more potent liquids (*Jungle Juice*, for example): They can melt plastics and ruin cameras, packs, and other things they leak onto. For camping trips to Scotland and Scandinavia, a head net (like beekeepers wear) weighs next to nothing and may save your sanity. Even if you don't expect this to be a problem, bring a small bottle or tube of repellent, just in case.

A Swiss Army Knife

Even if you're not camping, you should bring a Swiss Army knife, but you don't need to go for the giant versions that include the chain saw and the frying pan. The bottle opener is handy (twist-offs are less common in Europe), as are scissors.

A Sewing/Repair Kit

A small sewing kit can be worth its weight in platinum. Once again, you can put together your own. Include at least six needles, including some big ones for repairing your pack, as well as some dental floss and some serious wire for the same purpose. Also include thread, several safety pins, some buttons, and whatever else you can think of. The athletic tape in a first-aid kit is useful for repairs as well.

A Flashlight

A flashlight is surprisingly useful in dark hostels and is vital for camping; in fact, campers should bring two each. A mini-Maglight with two AA batteries is a good choice. Keep it someplace obvious in your pack, because you'll probably be looking for it in the dark. A little flashlight on a key ring is also very practical.

A Calculator

Some sort of calculator is useful mainly for quick currency conversions. It doesn't have to be anything special: a small $5-version is fine.

Sunscreen, Sunglasses, Lip Balm

One big bottle of factor fifteen sunscreen or better should be enough unless you plan on spending a lot of time at the beach. As with any other liquids, keep them in sealed plastic bags with the caps taped on until needed. Trust me on this one. Sunglasses should be sturdy and inexpensive, but not cheap. Bring a pair with real lenses, not just frames with colored glass, which can be worse than nothing. Sunglasses and sunscreen cost a bundle in touristy areas. A lip balm that includes sunscreen is best.

A Watch with Alarm or Travel Clock

Modern travel alarm clocks can be tiny – no bigger than a cassette tape. A moderately priced digital watch with an alarm and dual time (for timing those phone calls home) will also work if the alarm will wake you reliably – the sound is often not loud enough to stir a deep sleeper. You will have some early trains to catch, and buying a loud, reliable alarm clock is probably going to be money well spent.

A Sleep Sack

Sleep sacks are usually required in hostels, and they serve as bed linen, which hostels do not provide. A sleep sack is essentially a sleeping bag made from sheets, with a pillowcase attached. They are available direct from Hosteling International and discount travel agencies for about fifteen dollars, but you should skip those and make your own. Perfectly good ones can be made in less than an hour. Just fold a sheet over, sew up the long side and one of the short sides, flip inside out, and sew on a pillowcase – much cheaper than buying one, and a neat reminder of home. Sleep sacks with pictures of Barney or the Smurfs are considered very cool in Europe and will greatly impress the locals.

A Towel

This is a pet peeve of mine. You are much better off with a small, new, regular-weight bath towel than with one of those miserable little travel towels that soak up about as much water as a tissue and shed like a sheep dog. Sew a couple of solid cloth loops (old belt loops work well) to your towel so you can hang it from your backpack and let it dry while you're on the move.

Camera and Film

Obviously a personal choice, but if you're buying a camera for your trip, as with packs and shoes, going cheap is a recipe for heartache. As I write this, a 35mm point-and-shoot, which I bought for its low price of sixty dollars, is sitting in front of me. It broke after about three months, and ruined a roll of pictures that were worth more to me than the camera. Again, it's a good idea to buy quality; you won't regret it. On the other hand, a $1000 Nikon will be a constant worry, so don't go to the opposite extreme. I've found that the ideal camera for me is a pocket-sized point-and-shoot 35mm with a built-in zoom. These cameras are small, easy to carry, and run about $150–200. Also, their small size and concealability makes one look a bit less like a camera-toting tourist. If you already have a standard-sized camera, there's no problem with it, just be careful in crowds.

As far as film goes, it's *much* cheaper at home. Bring more than you think you'll need, and don't be surprised if you use it all. An extra battery is a good idea as well if yours is a bit old. If you don't use it, store it – and unused film – in the refrigerator when you get home.

Laundry Bags

Three or four plastic bags for separating dirty clothes, wrapping wet things, and so on, can be a godsend. They're also good for separating out things you won't need until a later part of your trip, and keeping them out of the way.

Toilet Paper

Don't laugh. In my scrapbook, I have several sheets of a gray substance. When asked to identify it, my friends guess that it is a type of mild abrasive, or perhaps tire-patching material. It is neither of these. It is, in fact, toilet paper from a Polish train station, and even today looking at it makes me cringe. But even this hellish stuff is superior to no paper at all, which is not uncommon in some bathrooms, particularly in public places. A good-sized wad of tissue at the bottom of a pocket or a daypack may some day save you from an unpleasant and undignified predicament. Remember, when others, less prepared than you, are in desperation, bargain mercilessly, especially if you've got the downy-soft product from home.

Bathroom Kit
Avoid "travel size" bathroom amenities, as they will run out and you will just have to buy more in Europe. An exception to this are small cans of shaving cream or gel, which hold a surprising amount. Just tape on the lids, or you may be in for a surprise.

Contact Lens Stuff/Glasses
The nightly chemical process familiar to contact-lens wearers is a mystery to me, but I did meet one guy who had spent two days searching for a particular type of solution in France. Even though the odds are good that gallons of whatever you need are no farther than the nearest pharmacy, brands may differ, and finding exactly what you're used to may be difficult. For simplicity, bring plenty of whatever solutions you need, and you may end up helping others.

When Theodore Roosevelt went charging up San Juan Hill with the Rough Riders, he had a dozen pairs of glasses: one in every possible pocket. This kind of planning is not a bad idea if you wear glasses. I would say three pairs are optimal, since it allows you to break one, lose one, and still keep going. Contact-lens wearers – bring more lenses than you think you will need.

Earplugs
Earplugs can be a sanity-saver for light sleepers in crowded hostels. The soft, foamy type work well (try at a

pharmacy), and you can sometimes get these free on your flight over the Atlantic. Try out your earplugs before leaving, because they can take some getting used to.

The Ever-Popular Universal Drain Plug

Every year hundreds of retired tennis and racket balls are reincarnated as these devices, used to plug stopper-less sinks for laundry and other chores. Just cut a tennis ball in half, and trim to the size desired. Use with smooth side down.

Documents

You should carry your passport with you at all times, because you may be asked to show it as identification. A passport is also necessary to cash travelers' checks, and may be needed to buy airline tickets.

If you lose your passport or if it is stolen, contact the nearest embassy immediately. They can issue you a temporary replacement. This process is much easier if you have a photocopy of the front pages of your passport. Carry at least one copy with you in a very safe place, like in a money belt, and have one copy at home in a very obvious place, like taped to the refrigerator door. If your passport gets lost, you will have a copy of the relevant information with you to take to your embassy. If the copy gets lost as well, the home front can fax you a copy of that same information.

You can do the same for credit cards, but don't carry this copy with you in Europe unless it is absolutely necessary. If your credit cards get stolen, they can be canceled by the person in the your home country. Other things you might want to copy and leave behind are travelers' check serial numbers, airline tickets, train passes, and any other documents you may lose.

You will be juggling a number of documents during your trip: a passport or identity card, train passes, airline tickets, and so on. I recommend keeping them out of the way as much as possible, preferably in some kind of folder or cover that is tied to the inside of your main pack.

Youth Hostel Membership Cards

Youth Hostel membership can be obtained along the way, but why not buy a card before you go and get one tiny worry off your mind? They're available from student travel offices or direct from the national organizations themselves (below) If possible, get a card, add a photo, and then laminate it, as an extra form of photo identification.

American Youth Hostels Association
PO Box 37613, Washington, DC 20013 (© 202-783-6161)
Canadian Hosteling Association
1600 James Naismith Dr, Suite 608,
Gloucester, Ontario K1B 5NH (© 613-748-5638)
Youth Hostels Association (Great Britain)
Trevelyan House, 8 St Stephens Hill,
St Albans, Herts AL1 2DY (© 0727-855-215)
Australian Youth Hostels Association
Level 3, 10 Mallett St, Camperdown, NSW 2050
(© 02-565-1699)
Youth Hostel Association of New Zealand,
PO Box 436, 173 Gloucester St, Christchurch 1
(© 03-379-9970).

Student and Other Identity Cards

In Europe, students receive a discount on anything that might be considered "educational," and on many things that aren't. Museums, tours, and other cultural attractions, often have a discounted admission or fare for those bearing an International Student Identification Card (ISIC). Nonstudents under 26 and teachers can get most of the same discounts with their own respective cards (the "GO 25" card and the International Teachers' Identity card). These are highly worth obtaining and can save you *megabucks* on an incredible number of things. Any student travel agent can either issue an ISIC on the spot or tell you where you can get one. You'll need a small photograph and proof that you're a full-time student. If you are a teacher or "youth," the same agencies can issue you your respective card. For seniors, proof that you are over 50 will get you discounts all over Europe.

When in Europe, and when buying tickets to get there, you should get into the habit of chanting "Is there a student discount?" every time you pull out some cash. This includes airlines, trains, ferries, museums, theaters, funeral parlors – everything, really. When in doubt, ask, and you will be amazed at the money you save.

If you are eligible for one of these cards and don't get one, you will kick yourself all across Europe. Call ☎1-800-GET AN ID for more information, or ask at any budget travel agent.

Extra "Passport" Photos

There are photo booths in seemingly every train station in Europe, so you can buy a set of photos when you get there, or just bring an extra set with you, as they weigh nothing and may be needed for city travel passes and such. You may also need some to give to that lovely European you meet during your travels. Sadly, I still have all four of mine. Regular photo booth pictures are fine, incidentally; don't pay those death-dealing passport photo places for more pictures than you have to.

International Driver's License

You can drive in most countries in Europe on your ordinary American or Canadian driver's license. However, in some countries you need an international driver's license, so if you think you might be driving while in Europe, one of these is worth obtaining. They're available from the AAA for ten bucks; you'll need a passport-sized photo and your (valid) driver's license. The process takes all of about ten minutes, and your license will be good for a year.

Train Timetables

The free timetable booklet that comes with your Eurail pass is fine if you are planning primarily to go to cities. For those not buying a pass, you can still get a timetable for free or for a nominal charge from any travel agent that sells rail passes. Don't ignore the printed information in this booklet, because some of it is very useful. These tables are quite flimsy, so replacing them when you're in a train station with a Eurail Aid office is a good idea.

The *Thomas Cook Railroad Timetable*, which gives information on seemingly every object that moves on any rail track in Europe, is of questionable value considering its weight and price ($30). However, if you are going in a group of two or more, you might get one for the group. Also, if you are planning to visit small towns and villages, you might want to invest in one. It certainly has tons of information; just make sure you need it all before buying it. It's also available from the Forsyth Travel Library – see "Maps", later in this chapter, for their number.

Hosteling Guides

Hosteling International puts out a book that gives details on every hostel in Europe, along with a map that shows their location. These two items are cheap, useful, and are absolutely essential for hostelers. They are especially useful for finding accommodations and/or planning trips off the beaten track, and for finding a hostel near a major city when all of the city accommodations are full. Both the book and the map should be available at any HI hostel in Europe. See Chapter 8 for more on hosteling.

Finally. . . a Journal, and some Pens

Bringing a book in which you can keep some sort of journal is a must. I guarantee you that you will be very glad you did after your trip, because the memories fade. My beaten-up old green book is one of the very last things I would part with. Use a journal not just for recording memories of your trip, but for recording good advice you get from other travelers, phone numbers, addresses, and so on. You should probably leave your address book at home, and take all the addresses you need in one of these. A small bound book will outlast a notebook by centuries, and may even end up amusing your grandchildren. Bound blank volumes are available at any office supply store or student union.

Optional Gear

The following equipment is optional, and most of it relates to camping. Don't make the mistake of bringing camping gear to give yourself "the option of camping." This stuff weighs a lot. Decide before you go if you're going to hostel or camp. This advice does not apply to those who are driving and thus less constrained by weight. In that case, by all means bring camping gear even if you intend to sleep indoors for most of your trip.

A Sleeping Bag

Obviously, a sleeping bag is mandatory if you are camping, and nice to have if sleeping indoors in rural areas and cool climates, as central heating has not made it to much of Europe's countryside. If you aren't going to be camping out, though, it's best to avoid the expedition-type down bags designed for winter in the Sierras. Those are too bulky and absolutely miserable to use, as you will drown in sweat in all but the coldest rooms. Go for minimum bulk, then go for minimum weight if hosteling. In general, a sleeping bag is only necessary if you will be spending time in the mountains, Northern Europe/Scandinavia, or other cold areas. For the big cities and for southern

Europe in the summer, a sleeping bag is not needed. Don't forget your sleep sack – many hostels will not allow you to use sleeping bags instead of sleep sacks on beds.

Cooking Gear

Some sort of cooking gear can be useful, and not just for campers. Many hostels have fully stocked kitchens, however, so go very light on what you bring. One small mess kit for two people should be fine. Cooking is work, but you'll probably eat better, and definitely eat cheaper, cooking for yourself.

Washing Liquid, Clothespins, a Line

Washing liquid is a necessary evil, since you'll need to wash things fairly regularly. Buy it in Europe. Clothespins are also very useful, as is a solid piece of line about twenty feet long that can be used for other things. I guarantee you will find other uses for it.

A Tent

A tent is obviously essential for campers, but unnecessary for hostelers. A tent weighs so much and takes up so much space that it is difficult to combine hostels and camping without cursing the damn tent every time you sleep in a hostel. If you are getting around in a car, on the other hand, a tent is a very nice thing to have with you, just in case.

For campers, unless you are planning a serious backcountry European trip, you probably won't need the same equipment you would in the mountains of the States or Canada. Your biggest problem will be rain, not cold, and a rain fly is essential, especially in Britain or Scandinavia – at any time of year. Also, remember that you will be spending a much longer time living in your tent than on a typical camping trip. A small tent for two or three people can be very unpleasant. Go for a larger volume than is absolutely necessary. If you have the option, bring a free-standing tent and leave the stakes and guy lines at home. Campgrounds can get crowded, and also those little bits and pieces can get lost very easily. For more information on tents, see the book by Harvey Manning mentioned in the "Luggage" section.

A Sleeping Pad

Campers should bring a thick sleeping pad, as much for insulation than for padding. A "thermarest" self-inflating type will be welcome in the mountains or in cold areas. If your pad of choice inflates in any way, bring a patch kit.

A Stove

The "Gaz" butane/propane stove is the king of the European campgrounds, and its little blue cylinders can be purchased all over Europe. If you have one of these stoves, remember that the airlines will go berserk if you put one of those little propane bomblets in your luggage. The same thing goes for the bottle of gas for liquid stoves. Fires are prohibited in most, if not all, European camp-grounds, so if you're camping, you'll definitely need a stove. Note that stoves are for campers only; you won't need one if hosteling.

A Compass

Absolutely essential for long-distance walkers, a compass is also surprisingly useful in large cities. Unless you have a gyroscope in your head, it is very easy to come out of a subway station disoriented, or to get lost in the maze of streets found in some old cities. A quick glance at your magic compass solves this problem, and will greatly impress your fellow travelers. Get one with a little mirror and a case, for both the protective case and the cute little mirror.

A Walkman

Only you know whether a Walkman is essential for you. If it is, be careful where you use it – people wearing head-phones are generally less aware of their surroundings, and thieves know this. The right tapes, though, can be a sure cure for homesickness.

A Whistle

A whistle is essential for long-distance walkers and campers who head off the beaten track. Also not a bad idea for single women, as part of a key chain or on a necklace, just in case.

A Deck of Cards

Cards are a great conversation-starter and time passer on long train rides.

Lou's Travel Key Chain

My own invention, tried and tested. The idea is that the best equipment is the stuff you have with you when you need it – everything else is worthless at that time. So, the key chain includes a micro Swiss Army knife, a tiny flashlight, a bottle opener, an army surplus mini can opener, and a small spoon. Truly pocket-sized and incredibly useful. I carry one everywhere, and I'd patent it if I could.

Pictures from Home

These are good to show to new friends, especially those in Eastern Europe, whose ideas about America may have come from episodes of *Dallas*, *Dynasty,* or *Baywatch*, and who may consider Canadians guilty by association. For those from Down Under, here's your chance to show the world your country is not just kangaroos, koalas, and sheep.

What Not to Bring

There are always things that you wish you hadn't taken – usually too late, when you're schlepping up to the eighth floor of your cheap pension. Rather than having to go through the agonies of off-loading stuff halfway through your trip, here are some pointers about what you really might not need.

Too Much Paper

Maybe it's just me, but I've found this a perennial problem. Those glossy brochures that I mentioned earlier are also given out by tourist offices in many of the countries you will visit, and are just as hard to part with. As before, copy any relevant information into a notebook, and then return the brochure or leave it at a hostel for others to read.

If you should minimize brochures, you should ultraminimize books. The paper in books is magically transformed into lead when enclosed in a backpack and hoisted to your shoulders. One guidebook per person (preferably different books if in a group), then maybe one book more. If you want to bring something to read in spare moments, bring cheap paperbacks that you can trade or give away.

Electrical Items

I'm sure you've heard the stories about melting clock radios, and the hair dryer that blacked out Paris when it was plugged in. Don't bother with this stuff. A battery-operated alarm clock is great, but hair dryers, electric razors, and other items will only be a pain. If you do bring electrical items, you must also bring an adapter, because European countries use 220 volt current (which may fry items designed for 115 volt operation), and the design of electrical outlets varies from country to country. If you simply must have an electrical item with you, or are planning a very long stay, consider buying what you need after you arrive, and selling it before you leave.

● ●

A FINAL PACKING IDEA
COURTESY OF AHN-ULD

The movie *Total Recall*, while disgustingly violent, did contain one very good idea for the European traveler. If you remember, Arnold Schwarzenegger had left himself a briefcase full of money, guns, explosives, disguises, and other handy stuff in case he got in trouble. Well, so can you. As insurance against a total disaster, such as a stolen backpack, why not put together a box of essentials like a change of clothes, back-up credit cards, an old camera, and anything you might need if a backpack or some of its contents were to be stolen or lost. Leave this box, unsealed, in the hands of someone reliable who can ship it to you should you need any or all of its contents. Nearly everything is more expensive in Europe than in North America, and if you have to do some heavy-duty replacement, the ability to quickly ship your sister's backpack, some clothes, mom's camera, a five-dollar watch, shoes, and so on, could save you a fortune. Why pay European prices to buy things you will only need for a few weeks? Antipodeans are, unfortunately, out of luck here.

At the very least, as mentioned earlier, you should leave a Xerox of the picture page of your passport, and also a Xerox of any credit cards you have, in case they need to be canceled. Also, if you are unsure that you can really travel as light as I recommend, why not put some of the things you think you might need in a box? If you ultimately do need them you can curse my stupid advice and send for them. I doubt if you will, though.

● ●

Maps

Spend a bit more on the best maps you can find and you won't regret it. As I said earlier, tourist offices are a good start. Any large bookstore will also have a map section.

Don't rely solely on the maps included in guidebooks, as they just can't do the job properly in such a small space.

The best planning map for rail travelers on the go is the *Rail Map of Europe* by Thomas Cook (available from the Forsyth Travel Library; ©1-800-367-7984). Though it's a bit too large for everyday use, this has every railroad from Moscow to Gibraltar shown, along with a wealth of other detail.

It's also handy to spot out-of-the-way places where trains don't go. There's also the Eurail train map that comes free with a pass, but this tends to start falling apart after about a week, so get two or three of these if you can. If you can't, reinforce the folds of the one you get with tape, and get a new one from a Eurail Aid office while on the move. These offices are found in many large train stations, and their locations are listed on the Eurail map. This map has some good information on its reverse side that is well worth reading – stuff like language tips, details on train station facilities, Eurail discounts, and so on.

Guidebooks

This may seem an obvious item to bring, but I have met several people who didn't take a guidebook to Europe. They weren't sure if they would need one and were sure that they could buy one easily in Europe if they did. Generally, I met them when they tried to buy my guidebook.

Needless to say, you should bring one. I have traveled both with and without a guidebook, and it is much easier and simpler to have one with you. If you lose yours, you can fake it for a while by using tourist offices to locate places to stay, major sights, and so on, but if you get an opportunity to buy another, you should. There are some travelers who disagree with me, who say guidebooks can become law books, and travelers tend to follow them as if they contained mandatory statutes on what to see and where to stay. There is some truth in this, and it is indeed possible to follow your book too slavishly. However, if that becomes a problem, just stick your book in the bottom of your pack and forget about it until you really need it. On the other hand, if you do need a guide and don't have one, you will be out of luck.

There are an incredible number of guidebooks available for every possible tiny corner of Europe – the amount is truly unbelievable. Some thoughts on this literary tidal wave:

◆ If you only intend visiting two or three countries, it is worth the expense and bulk to buy separate books on each, rather than a guide to all of Europe that is full of information you won't use. For example, Rough Guide's Europe has 118 pages on Italy. Their Italy book covers the same territory in about a thousand pages. For someone who is going to spend a week in Italy, 118 pages is about enough to cover the very basics, and point the way to some of the highlights of Rome, Florence and Venice. For someone planning on spending a month, wandering from Milan to Palermo and on to Sardinia, a thousand pages would be a wise investment. If you're not sure where you want to go but intend to visit more than three countries, get a Europe guide and you won't regret it.

❖ The book you choose will be a very important part of your trip, and you will use it just about every day. Check a few out of the library, or at least take an hour in a bookstore to compare the various options. There are marked differences among the guides available.

❖ Always use the most up-to-date version of the guidebook you prefer. Trying to save a few dollars by using an old version is a very poor idea.

❖ All of the books described below, whether I care for them or not, represent a huge amount of work and information gathering. Before going, no matter what book you buy, sit down and read all the opening pages and the section on the first country you will visit. You will find an astounding amount of useful information that you might never have suspected was in there. As always, I learned that the hard way. If you have a question, try your guidebook and see if it is answered somewhere.

❖ Which is the best guidebook? As always, I can only report from my experiences; whether they are applicable to you is for you to decide. Please note that dishing dirt on another author's work is a tender issue when writing a book, and most authors simply praise one another in a never-ending circle. As I write this, nobody has raved about me yet, so I don't feel the obligation to rave about anybody else. Let me state at the outset that this book is published by Rough Guides, so you might want to take that into account. They certainly haven't put the heat on me to push their books (and wouldn't succeed if they did), but you should know the facts.

Berkeley Guides

Berkeley Guides, who publish a guide called *Europe on the Loose* and a number of single country guides, is the new kid on the block. Their guides are written primarily by students of the University of California, Berkeley, and are aimed squarely at the student budget traveler. They are clearly intended to be direct competition for Let's Go, which dominates that market. Berkeley Guides tries to carve a niche for itself by being more irreverent, more youth-oriented and, to be honest, more politically correct than the next guide. ("Two trees are planted for every one sacrificed for our books.") Although cleverly disguised as a student production, however, the book is actually a product of Fodor's Travel Publications, which has been a heavyweight in traditional guidebooks for years. Their Europe guide itself is pretty average: it has some nice color maps, but has the shortest planning section I've ever seen. It could work for someone who wants an "all Europe in one book" guide that is not Let's Go.

Frommer's

If Berkeley Guides is the new kid, Frommer's is the grand old man; Arthur Frommer pretty much invented budget travel in Europe for non-Europeans with his revolutionary *Europe on Five Dollars a Day*. The current version is entitled *Europe '95 on $50 a Day*, which is a statement in itself on what has happened to budget travel over the years. This guide, however, only covers 31 major cities and the areas around them and, like the rest of the series, has been somewhat overtaken among budget travelers by other, younger series. The information is not particularly budget-oriented, and the presentation is poor. Basically, there are better guides, especially for travelers on a tight budget.

Let's Go

Let's Go Europe is the guidebook of choice for the majority of young Americans and Canadians traveling in Europe. Let's Go is written by Harvard undergraduate students, so consider the source when opinions are expressed about politics and countries. Let's Go also publishes a number of single country guides.

Let's Go Europe has a useful color section of metro and city maps; it is partially updated every year; and, if you want to meet your compatriots abroad, remember that more young Americans and Canadians have this book than all others combined. On the downside, it covers 31 countries in one book, and so covers each country without very much depth. You may also find the fact that so many North Americans are carrying it a disadvantage, as hostels mentioned in *Let's Go Europe* fill up very quickly.

Lonely Planet

Lonely Planet publishes guides to nearly every country in the world. Originally specializing in Asia and relatively remote areas, they now publish five different multi-country guides to Europe, as well as large single-country guides. They do not, however, publish a single all-Europe guide, focusing instead on regions such as Western, Central, and Eastern Europe. This could be a drawback: If you're traveling widely, you'll probably need at least two books. As for their strengths, they include maps of major cities, with places to stay, banks, post offices, etc, shown; they include mini language dictionaries included in the country background sections, as well as brief but interesting histories and background articles. Books are updated every few years.

Rough Guides

Rough Guides is a British company, and therein lies its major strength as far as Europe goes. It has a home field advantage over other guidebooks, as continental Europe is only a ferry ride away. They publish individual guides to most European countries, as well as a thirty-country

Europe guide with some color maps. Most books are updated every two years, some every three. I really can't say much more about Rough Guides that you would believe; as I said, they publish this book.

Choosing a Guidebook

I can say that if you are looking for a one-book guide to Europe, you should compare the Rough Guide to the Let's Go, Berkeley Guides and as many Lonely Planets as you might need. In my mind Berkeley Guides is somewhat inferior to the others, and Let's Go is handicapped by the fact that nearly everyone has one. Consider the guides yourself, and then choose whichever you think will be best for you.

● ●

READ YOUR GUIDEBOOK – HOW I LEARNED

It was late, I was in Munich, and every hostel was full. My only option was "The Tent" – two big circus-type tents, one with beds and one for those who wanted to save 3 marks by sleeping on the floor. (This place is an experience, by the way; a throwback to the Sixties in many ways). I needed to phone for directions, so I bought a banana to get change (70 pfennigs). I called the number given in my guidebook (30 pfennigs), got a recording giving those directions, but wasn't ready to copy them. I wandered around the station, bought some candy (50 pfennigs) and got some more change. Back at the phone, I wickedly tried to use a foreign coin which looked like it might work in the phone (10 pence). It didn't. In exasperation I threw a whole 1 mark coin in, only to have it get stuck behind the 10 pence (1 mark). I went to get more change (50 pfennigs) and changed phones. I called again (1 mark) and got my directions, half-an-hour after I started. As I was closing my book, I noticed the directions to "The Tent" – in my guidebook, right under the phone number.

● ●

CHAPTER FIVE

GETTING THERE

Okay, guys, this is where some money is going to be saved if you work at it. That airline ticket is going to be a major chunk of your budget, and, as we all know, airline fares are determined by some form of black magic unknown to the flying public. If you are smart and patient, you can pay about half of what the guy on your left is paying for the same flight, and a third of that woman on your right.

I am old enough to barely remember when airlines were really airlines, and planes were airliners, and travel by air was something special. It was more expensive then, but a hell of a lot more gracious and enjoyable. Traveling by air today is a contact sport, bordering on open warfare. Fares are raised for no discernible reason, discounted the next week, and always jacked up ruthlessly before Thanksgiving and Christmas. Welcome to the Nineties. Flying today is often miserable, and if you're going to be miserable for that day it takes you to make the hop across North America and/or the Atlantic and/or Pacific, you may as well go cheaply. Doing this is going to take some looking around well before you go – like three months before, if possible. That's the time to start if you're serious, and read the travel section of your local paper, or the nearest big city daily, to keep an eye on things.

The factors you will be juggling are the following:

1. Price
2. Changeability
3. Refundability
4. How long a stay
5. Stand-by or reserved
6. Point of entry to Europe
7. Point of exit from Europe
8. Which airline
9. Arrival time in Europe
10. Other restrictions

First Steps

The first step is to figure out where you want to fly out of and where you want to start out in Europe. For Americans, Los Angeles, San Francisco, Dallas-Fort Worth, Atlanta, and New York, either JFK or Newark, will usually be cheapest, especially JFK/Newark. It may be worth bumming a ride to one of these places, even from a good distance. Those arriving from other countries don't have as much of a choice. Montreal, Toronto, Auckland, Sydney, and Melbourne are by far the largest gateways. The major, and probably the cheapest, points of entry to Europe are London, Paris, and Frankfurt. Those wishing to fly to Rome will probably have to go through Milan.

A word of advice: On a first trip, the first day overseas can be overwhelming, especially if you are alone. Flying into a country where you speak the language will make things less stressful. Despite the long lines and despotic immigration officers, London might not be a bad place to start. London is also a good place to start for the cheap travel options available from there to Greece or points beyond the European continent. Also, since Eurail passes are not valid in Britain, many people go to London first or last to avoid wasting valuable pass time during their time spent there. But if your dream of going to Europe has always included getting on a plane and then getting off in Paris or Rome, then by all means fly to those airports and show 'em who's boss. It's your trip.

After you've chosen where to leave from and fly into, the next step is to establish an upper limit on your fare. This is easily done by calling major airlines on their toll-free numbers, and waiting until their overworked operators answer. When they do answer, ask for the price of the cheapest fare from your exit point to your initial destination, and inquire about any restrictions, advance purchase requirements, etc. Then ask if there is anything cheaper to any other city in Europe you are willing to fly into, and/or from any other city you are willing to fly out of. It pays to be nice to the person who answers by the way. He or she will have access to tons of information and may go to greater lengths for you with just a little courtesy on your part.

Barring a fare war or major sale, what you will get from the airlines is their published, economy-class, two-week advance purchase fare. This is now your upper limit. Anybody can get these just by phoning an airline and asking. You are now working down from that price – if someone offers you a "special deal" that costs more than that, hang up. You should find all of the airlines to be very close, if not identical, on the price of these fares. A warning for older travelers: One discount that *isn't* is the "senior citizen's fare" on airlines. This is usually a 10 percent savings on fares sold directly by the airline. But as you will soon see, tickets from budget travel agents can cost hundreds of dollars less than these "discount" fares

The next stop is the Sunday travel section of the nearest large metropolitan newspaper, and the local "alternative" newspaper, if any. The major daily papers in all of the cities mentioned above are good, as are the *Village Voice*, *LA Weekly*, and *San Francisco Bay Guardian*. If you're near a major university, you might want to check out a copy of the school paper. In all of these, you should see many small ads for unbelievably priced tickets. Since they are so unbelievable, you should not believe them. What they are good for, however, is a lower limit; you probably won't be able to beat the fares advertised unless you are very fortunate. So there you have it – your fare should lie between the two extremes. The challenge now, of course, is to get as close to the bottom as possible.

Travel agents

Travel agents connect those who have some form of "travel product," such as an airline seat, a hotel room or a space on a tour, with the potential buyer. A travel agent is a resource that you should at least consider; they can provide you with far more information than you could pos-sibly gather on your own, and barring a major fare war, you'll never find the cheapest airfare without using some kind of agent. The price structure for agents is set up so that using an agent will not cost you more than booking a ticket yourself.

Travel agents can be a blessing or a curse, and it is up to you, if you choose to go this route, to find one that you feel comfortable with. They can always make travel easier for you, and they can usually make it cheaper, but it is up to you to make decisions based on the information they provide. Your agent should assist you, not direct you.

As with any major purchase, shop around. Don't simply go to the local travel bureau and assume that they will give you the best service and get you the best price. Before going to an agent, you should have at least a basic idea of where and when you want to go. Don't just walk in and say: "I want to go to Europe, but I don't know where." Make it easy on them by deciding when you want to leave, where you want to start out in Europe, and how long you want to stay. Work out a rough itinerary, and you can both take it from there.

When using an agent, go with one that deals with budget travel and/or students regularly, preferably daily. Any agent will be happy to fly you to Europe, but if they're used to booking ten thousand dollar/one-month luxury trips they may not be able to serve your needs. You certainly don't want them to reinvent the budget travel wheel in booking your trip.

Some agencies deal almost exclusively with students and/or budget travelers, and with these places the distinction between travel agency and consolidator (see below) can sometimes become blurry. If you are booking an ultra-cheap seat somewhere, you should be prepared to give the budget/student agent you use the same scrutiny that I advise in the next paragraph.

Consolidators

We all know what a travel agent is; a consolidator is similar. These places, also known as bucket shops, deal in seats the airlines don't think they can sell at normal prices. Rather than sell these seats in their name, which would irritate customers paying full fare, airlines release blocks of them to consolidators for resale. These guys then sell them to travelers who are willing to take the time and effort to seek them out.

Consolidators are the people advertising those unbelievable prices, and even if they are almost never as low as advertised, they can still be very cheap. They can be cheap for a number of reasons: student discounts, lower than expected bookings, inconvenient times, off-season departures, flying on strange airlines, flying into smaller or more inconvenient airports (like London Gatwick instead of London Heathrow), long delays in changing planes, a mandatory stopover in Angola, whatever. If you are persistent, you will probably be able to find something where you want to go, when you want to go, at a couple hundred dollars below the airline's published fare. So get on the phone and start calling the places in the paper, and see what they can do for you. Do a lot of calling around, write down whatever they tell you in great detail (you'll definitely forget some of what they say if you don't), and don't be afraid to ask questions. Some pointers for dealing with agents or consolidators:

◇ If you are a student, with an ISIC card, mention that up front.

◇ Round-trip tickets are almost always cheaper than two single tickets. In fact, because most single fares are based on half of the full-price round-trip fare, they can cost more than some discount round trips. Hard to believe, but often true. Don't get a single from home and expect to get a cheap single out of London. Get your return ticket from Europe before you go, unless you have no firm date of return.

◇ Never be pressured into buying a ticket right away, even if they tell you it is "the last one left in the world." If that were the case, they wouldn't need to pressure you to buy it. Don't be rushed into anything. On the other hand, don't get an excellent deal that works perfectly for you and then wait a week for no reason.

◇ When offered a ticket, keep in mind the ten factors mentioned earlier. Ask if it is refundable (it probably won't be if it's cheap). Ask how long it is valid for. Ask how much it would cost to change the European departure city. And ask about any restrictions they may have "forgotten" to tell you about.

❖ One possibility to consider is a stopover flight, where you stop for a few days in another European city on the way to your final destination. These are usually found on the big European national carriers, and can sometimes be done at no extra charge, or for as little as $50–100 per stop. As an example, *Icelandair* does a three-day stopover in Iceland on its way to continental Europe.

❖ Never pay cash if you can avoid it. Use a credit card, and after you have the ticket in hand, call the airline and see if it is a valid ticket (check destination, date, one way or round trip, price, etc.). As I write this, the radio is reporting on a group of teachers from California that went to Zimbabwe, only to discover that their "round-trip" tickets were actually one way. Not one of them checked. Don't make the same mistake. If the ticket is bogus in some way, cancel the charge, and call the police. If you don't have a credit card, and can't use someone else's, be up front. Tell your agent that you want to confirm your ticket with the airline, and get all the details they would use to get the ticket. Then call the airline and ask if the ticket could be issued at the price you're paying. An hour of wariness could save you hundreds of dollars and weeks of headaches.

❖ Walk out of any place that demands cash in advance. Don't even look back.

❖ Don't buy a ticket over the phone if you can possibly go to the office itself. If the office is a basement with two phone lines and a desk, it may not be there when something goes wrong with your ticket in three months.

❖ Ideally, you want to arrive in Europe early in the day. You definitely do not want to be getting off a plane and then have to look for housing in the middle of the night. Remember that you will have to clear customs and immigration upon arrival; it may take as much as two or three hours from your landing time for you to get to your accommodations. Take this into account when planning your arrival time.

❖ Be aware of the different travel seasons airlines work by. Flights will be cheapest between the end of October and the end of March – the low season. They will be moderately expensive in the so-called shoulder seasons of April/May and September/October; and they will be most expensive during the June–August period. As the spring/summer travel season approaches, expect the available seats to dry up. Start poking around in February. If you are reading this in May, get to work now.

❖ The more shops you visit or call, the more comfortable you will be with the whole process. Start early, have your plans together, don't let yourself be pressured, and you will be fine.

Round-the-World Tickets

You will notice, once in Europe, the large number of Aussies and Kiwis who seem to be traveling on a perpetual tour of the world for next to nothing. This is not just perception – the relative isolation of those two countries makes a quick trip to and from Europe out of the financial question. However, quirks of the airline industry can make it cheaper to travel around the world than simply back and forth to Europe. For example, a QANTAS round-trip ticket from Sydney to London costs around $1500, bought directly from the airline. Meanwhile, an itinerary of London-Nairobi-Delhi-surface travel to Kathmandu-Bangkok-Singapore-Bali-Perth-surface travel to Melbourne-Auckland-Los Angeles-London is about the same price, excluding the cost of surface travel. No wonder so many from down under travel this way. Travelers from other countries should consider this option too – some RTW tickets may be had for as little as one thousand dollars. Why not return to America via Hong Kong? Many of the student and budget travel agencies listed in *Basics* #5 can put together a RTW trip or refer you to someone who can.

If you're planning a round-the-world trip from down under that hits the United States before Europe and other points east, be aware of another money-saver. Backpacks, camping equipment, hiking boots, and other gear are much cheaper in the States. Besides seeing the spectacular beauty of my homeland, you can save about 50 percent on such items by buying them here. Get catalogs from the suppliers listed in *Basics #7* for some comparison shopping.

Charters, Courier Flights, and Other Options

During your search for a seat you may hear rumors, or see ads, for incredible deals based on courier flights or charters. Beware. In the travel industry, as elsewhere, there is no free lunch. Courier flights match travelers who want to go somewhere with companies or individuals who need something, usually documents, transported by air. The courier company sells you a cheap ticket in exchange for you sacrificing some or all of your luggage allowance. The amount of these discounts, in accordance with supply and demand, dries up during early and late summer, when many students are happy to save a small amount. Also, most courier flights require a return trip within a certain length of time, usually a few weeks. If this interests you, search the phone book and small ads. Be sure to get a firm commitment from a courier company before gambling your trip on this option.

Charters are great when they work, and absolute hell when they don't. Expect older planes packed to the rafters with people, and poor in-flight service. (Actually, that doesn't sound a whole lot different from the major airlines, does it?) At any rate, the big worry with charters is whether or not they will leave as scheduled. The difference between a plane 95 percent full and one that's 99 percent full may be the difference between profit and loss for the charter operator, and a flight may be delayed for "maintenance" while the last few seats are sold. Some charter companies are as reliable as the major airlines, whereas others are operating at the edge of bankruptcy and may disappear with your money without trace. Get a neutral opinion, such as from a travel agent you are not giving money to, on the reliability of a charter company before you hand them several hundred dollars.

CHAPTER SIX

(ALMOST) BEING THERE

After all the planning and purchasing, it's finally getting close to departure time. There are only a few last-minute details to consider. I will also belabor you with some personal advice in this chapter. Actually heading out for Europe can be a stressful process, and I hope this advice makes the trip as smooth as possible.

❖ On international flights you should call your airline within 72 hours of your departure time to confirm that you will indeed be going and to check for any schedule changes. Some airlines may offer your seat for sale if you don't, although this supposedly is rare.

❖ Definitely call ahead and make a reservation for your first few nights in Europe. The last thing you want to do on arrival is look for housing. Also, you'll probably be wiped out from the trip. A room in a small pension or cheap hotel, as opposed to a dorm bed in a hostel, might make for a quicker recovery. See Chapter 11 for more on international calls.

❖ When you make your reservation, get explicit directions to the place you will be staying, including metro stops, cross streets, prominent landmarks in the area, etc. Once again, make it easy for yourself on that first day.

❖ If you plan on meeting another traveler while in Europe, be aware that this can be difficult. Try and pick a very specific location (such as "touching the statue of Goya outside the Prado in Madrid") and not "at the Eiffel Tower." Don't plan to meet outdoors at night or in a place that charges admission. Also, it's a good idea to have a number, even one at home, that both of you can call to leave messages, in case plans change or you miss each other. Another small fruit of bitter experience. . .

❖ If you live alone, don't forget all of the standard "going-on-a-trip" things to do: empty the refrigerator, stop the paper, make arrangements for plants and pets, put a vacation hold on your mail at the post office, etc. As a personal request, please take special care with pets. Never, ever, just lock a cat out (let alone a dog), with a few pounds of dry food in a bowl.

❖ If you have a car, especially an old one, you might want to fill the gas tank and disconnect the battery before letting it sit for two months. Or have someone drive it every week or so, if you trust your friend not to take your faithful sled on a road trip.

❖ Arrive at the airport at least two hours prior to your takeoff time, especially if you are taking a non-US airline or a charter. New security regulations have increased the time needed for check-in. A frantic dash to the airport, let alone a missed flight, is a poor way to start any trip. Better to get the lines over with and relax.

❖ Parking at most airports is very expensive and not very secure. If at all possible, get a ride from someone.

❖ Practice your money-changing skills by purchasing about fifty dollars worth of the currency of the first country you will visit. That way you can skip the line at the airport change counter in Europe and avoid its lousy exchange rate; it's also a good backup should you turn up and find everything closed. Just like in Europe, try a major bank first. As a last resort, try the change booth at your home airport.

❖ You may not know this, but airport food is expensive poison, designed to weaken your system so the dreaded airline food can finish you off. Bring your own food with you, and you'll eat much better and much cheaper.

❖ The air you breathe while on an airplane is drier than any air found naturally anywhere on earth. As a result, it is very easy to become dehydrated on long flights, which can cause headaches, nausea, and other discomforts. Bring a big bottle of water with you, and drink it all during the flight. You'll need it. It's also a good idea to steer clear of alcohol and carbonated drinks. The best way to deal with the inevitable jet lag is to try to get in synch with the time difference as soon as possible. For example, if you arrive at midday local time, you should attempt to stay awake until reasonably late in the evening rather than taking a nap in the afternoon.

❖ Upon arrival in Europe, hit the bathroom and get a drink before getting in the endless customs line upon arrival, or even before commencing the sometimes endless wait at the carousel for your luggage if you've checked it. This, of course, is another reason for packing light, as those with only carry-on items will be able to skip the luggage claim area and go directly to customs, leaving the heavy packers fuming as the customs lines grow longer.

❖ When and if you get to England, obvious as it may seem, slow down and actively practice looking both ways when crossing streets. The British habit of driving on the left runs counter to years of ingrained habits for most tourists, and every year several are hit by cars. Near misses abound, including several that involved me. Though Brits may snigger at this advice, this is not a matter of intelligence. Winston Churchill, on a visit to New York, was nailed by a taxi after looking the wrong way. Some time ago some genius had the brilliant idea of painting signs on the crosswalks telling you which way to look. Follow these directions; they saved my life once.

A Microcourse in European Culture

A number of guidebooks list some of the customs and social idiosyncrasies of the various European countries, to help travelers avoid offending their hosts. In general, this is a good idea, but I sincerely doubt that many travelers will be able to pull a particular custom out of their memory when the occasion demands. The following general advice should work in all European countries, and all countries in the world, for that matter. Ninety-nine percent of it is common sense, but it does bear repeating. I apologize for any tone of self-righteousness, and I admit that I have violated many of these rules myself.

◆ Never simply speak English to someone and expect them to answer you in English. I find this extremely rude. How would you react if someone visiting your hometown started talking to you in Swedish and expected to be answered? Always ask, in the local language, if a person speaks English. If they don't, say "Thank you" in the local language anyway. See *Basics* #10 for some simple phrases in most European languages.

◆ Beginning a sentence with "please" will work wonders. "Please, where is the train station?" sounds a whole lot better than "Where is the train station?"

◆ If you are holding a conversation in English, it is a nice gesture to thank the person for speaking your language, and thereby making the conversation possible. Whenever I have done this it has been appreciated greatly by the person I thanked.

◆ Handshakes are very common in Europe, particularly in southern European countries. Shaking hands on meeting and departing, even when you see someone several times a day, is common.

◆ Greeting a storekeeper on entry, and saying good-bye on exit, is standard all over Europe.

◆ Canadians will not face the occasional scrutiny that some Americans will receive from some Europeans, other than the occasional questioning as to just why their government requires them to wear maple leaves when they travel. Australians may find the image of "Crocodile" Dundee has preceded them, while Kiwis may find that no image has preceded them, and may wish to carry a world map to point out the location of the "Land of the Silver Fern."

❖ In my experience, Americans are perceived in Europe as friendly, monolingual, a bit loud, and usually in a hurry. There are reasons for all of these perceptions. If I could give advice, it would be the following: Try to blend in wherever you happen to be. Try not to change the place you are visiting with your presence, as with, for example, a loud conversation in English in a cathedral or museum. Slow down a bit when dealing with the people and especially in restaurants, as most Europeans expect to be left alone for long periods while eating. Trying to hurry someone or making a scene never helps a situation. There are some countries in Europe, which I won't name, whose traveling citizens could benefit from this advice as well.

❖ As an American, you may be called upon to explain some obscure point of American foreign policy, such as our terribly high tariffs on Danish ham, or why America doesn't bomb Bosnia just when and where the Europeans want them to. I once spent two hours explaining to a German student that, no, the United States did not pay Saddam Hussein to invade Kuwait so that America could make money from the contracts to rebuild Kuwait City. Don't argue with people who treat you as if you make American foreign policy.

❖ You are, whether you like it or not, a representative of your country when you are abroad. Treat the people you meet with respect and sensitivity, don't condescend, and you will be fine.

❖ Far more important than any language skill or knowledge of local customs is a positive, friendly attitude, and, especially, a smile. In every culture on earth a smile means the same thing, and cannot be taken for anything but an expression of friendship. In every culture I've been exposed to, it has worked wonders.

Over to you . . .

At this point, the planning, packing, and buying are over (and so is the cultural sermon). You've got your passport, tickets, and rail pass in hand, your stuff is all packed, your plans are more or less made, and you're ready to go. There's a 747 out there with your name on it, and Europe is yours for the taking. The rest of this book concerns the practical things you need to know about travel in Europe, because that's where you're going. Congratulations.

CHAPTER SEVEN

GETTING AROUND

So here you are, in Europe at last. I hope that this chapter includes all you need to know to get around easily. You have a major ally in doing so – the local tourist authority. Most European cities and countries benefit greatly from the tourist trade, and they have spent large amounts of money to make things easy on you. Most countries have a large network of tourist offices, sometimes in the smallest town or village, and this is usually an incredibly valuable resource. They can do a lot more for you than simply hand you a map and direct you to a hostel, but to get full value you must ask. The office in the main train station may be a bit rushed in August, so be prepared with some questions, such as (1) are there any festivals or celebrations planned in the local area any time soon, or any planned in the region in the next week or so? (2) is anything on the normal tourist trail closed? (3) is there any attraction that you personally recommend I see, perhaps something off the tourist trail? Use these people, and be polite with them – they are often overworked during the summer.

Along with tourist offices, there are also train information offices that can help you tremendously in your traveling around. If a question is not answered in this chapter, or you have a question about a specific trip or service, ask at one of these offices, and I guarantee that you will be helped on your way. Since you will probably be taking public transportation from the airport to wherever you are staying, information on getting around cities will be presented first, followed by information on intercity and international travel.

Getting Around Cities

The great news is that you are finally in Europe. The not-so-great news is that you are now in an airport. Obviously you need to get out of there as fast as you can, and head for whatever accommodations you have reserved. I have to say that very few issues seem to worry prospective travelers more than moving around foreign cities on public transport. It really should not. Remember that you are not the first person to come to Paris without knowing how to speak French. If only for their own convenience, transportation authorities all over Europe do their best to help foreign visitors. Read the section below and with a little practice you will be well on your way to becoming an expert.

One of the really nice aspects of traveling in Europe is the incredible public transportation that is available in the major cities. Most European cities have combinations of subways (metros), streetcars (trams), and buses that shame the best in the United States, or anywhere else in the world for that matter. Paris and London, in particular, have extremely convenient and extensive subway and bus systems. Since most of the famous sights, museums, and monuments are usually clustered in the centers of the larger cities, walking, combined with riding the bus or metro, is an easy way to see a multitude of attractions quickly.

All this convenience comes at a price, however, and intra-city transport can be a surprisingly large expense. Buying tickets one at a time is almost *never* the cheapest way to travel. In major cities like London, Rome, Madrid, and Paris, take a serious look at how much moving around you are going to do, and see if a day or week pass makes sense. In Central London, for example, a one-way trip on the tube costs £1, at least in the central zone, while an all-day, unlimited travel pass for Central London costs £2.80. Even though, at nearly five dollars, the day pass is expensive, it is a good deal for someone who is planning on packing a lot into a day, especially those who want to go out in the morning and afternoon, come back to where they're staying, and then go back out in the evening. A weekly pass, which requires a small photo, at £13 is even cheaper per day. If you're staying a week and aiming to see a lot of the city, it may make the most sense.

Other metros sell books of ten tickets at huge discounts versus the cost of single tickets. (Paris sells one-shots at F7.50 each, or ten tickets for F45, so the last four rides are free). As a general rule, you can expect a weekly pass in a major European city to pay for itself in a five-day stay, or after four days of hard use. The usual tip parade on city transport:

❖ Metros (subways) can be confusing at first, but will be a piece of cake in a few days. Lines are either named (as in London), designated by a letter or number, or simply named according to the final stop on the line. Usually the various lines are also color-coded. Trains run back and forth on each colored line, and never change colors. To get from one line to another you must stop at a station that serves both lines, walk to another platform and grab another train. Trains are generally named, and announced in the stations, according to the name of the last station on their line in the direction they are going; in most cities trains carry signs showing the name of this last station in their front window. When in doubt about how to get somewhere, ask somebody. Most locals, as well as your fellow travelers, will be glad to help you.

❖ If you're not sure whether you're going in the right direction, watch as the stations go by. It should be obvious what direction you're going in very quickly. Don't start reading a newspaper and end up across town in Berlin, as I did.

❖ Metro tickets can usually be purchased at the station itself. Bus and tram tickets, often one and the same, can often be purchased from news kiosks and tobacco shops, as well as from the drivers themselves. Most drivers, however, cannot change large bills. Tourist offices sometimes sell daily and weekly passes, and if they don't they can always tell you where to get one.

❖ Most European buses, trams, and some metros operate on the honor system; you're supposed to cancel your own ticket, often with little punching machines in each car or bus. If you don't see locals doing this, it's because they have monthly passes. From time to time you may be asked to produce your ticket by an inspector. Failure to show a canceled ticket (for that day) can result in a stiff fine on the spot ($15–40, depending on the city) and rude comments from the inspector concerning your morality. The most ferocious inspectors are in Germany, while the clear winners for the wimpiest are in Amsterdam, where locals stare in shock if any tourist pays for his tram ride.

❖ Because of the system described above, you often do not have to enter a bus or tram through the front door. Enter anywhere, stamp your ticket, and you're good to go.

❖ Within a given city there are usually myriad metro/bus/tram transfer privileges. Your guidebook should detail these, but an inquiry at the tourist office is advisable as well.

◇ Most metro systems give out free pocket-sized maps, which can save pulling out your guidebook or unfolding a city map every few minutes.

◇ Though buses and trams are slower than metros, they offer a much better view, and give you a feel for the cities that contain all those museums and monuments.

Moped and Bicycle Rental

Almost every European city and town has a bicycle rental agency somewhere, which should be listed in your guidebook. Some of these places allow bikes to be dropped off at any of their offices throughout a city or region, allowing some great day trips. In Holland, Belgium and France it is often possible to rent bikes at train stations. As I said in Chapter 2, be careful about using bikes in cities, even if you see the locals doing so, and try to get a helmet. For those who don't want to bring a hard shell helmet with them, the kind made from several flexible tubes is better than nothing, although not by much.

Where you should be careful about a bicycle, you should treat a moped as if it were a sworn enemy. Mopeds are a ton of fun, but can be very dangerous. Once a friend of mine and I were in Barcelona and noticed a large number of beautiful women wearing neck braces and large bandages on their arms and legs. Our waiter explained that these were the result of Spanish vacationers using mopeds during their holidays. Renting a moped is easy, while renting a helmet (or a safe helmet) can be difficult. Consider the risks carefully, and watch out for the other guy.

Taxis

For some reason, a large percentage of taxi drivers everywhere, with the notable exception of London, are scheming, lying crooks who see impoverished travelers as little more than walking piggy banks to be emptied as quickly as possible. This is particularly true in France, Italy, Greece, and especially in Prague, where cabbies have a reputation for thieving and violence akin to that of the Mafia in Sicily. Most of us poor travelers will go months without seeing the inside of a cab, but here's the scoop if one becomes necessary.

- ❖ Single women, as always, beware. Don't just get in a cab and tune out your surroundings. Follow the progress of your driver, and if it looks as if he's going somewhere other than where you told him, speak up or get out at a stop. Silence is the best response to suggestive comments.
- ❖ At airports there is almost always public transport available. If someone, especially a taxi driver, tells you there isn't, look for yourself. Don't let yourself be pushed toward the taxi stand by a "helpful" porter or airport employee – he may be getting a cut of your fare.
- ❖ No meter, no ride. Avoid cabs with no meter, or one that is "broken." In Eastern Europe, this may be difficult, as meters may date from before the fall of the Iron Curtain, and therefore calculate very cheap fares. In these countries, and especially Russia, almost anyone with a car is willing to negotiate a ride for a fee. Just make sure you agree on the fee in advance; write it down if necessary. Again, if you can't do this, then don't take the ride.

❖ Find out what a cab ride should cost from someone who knows, if possible, and offer a bit less than this if the cabbie refuses to use the meter and you absolutely have to use his cab.

❖ If you agree on a fare, and the cabbie tries to charge you more at the end of your ride, hand him the amount you agreed on and walk away. This is less likely to happen if you were firm and clear in stating the fare at the beginning.

❖ Your average cabbie speaks bits and pieces of more languages than your average diplomat. If he pretends not to be able to agree on a fare because of his lack of English, beware.

❖ If the taxis in an area seem a bit sleazy, don't put your pack in the trunk if you can avoid it. If you have to use the trunk, get your pack out first, then pay the driver.

❖ Don't sacrifice safety to stay on a budget. If you arrive after dark, especially in a big city, don't walk the streets with a backpack just to save a couple of bucks. This is especially true for women traveling alone. A cab is a bargain in this situation.

❖ Finally, don't leave London without riding in a Black Cab. There's enough room in those things to house (or start) a small family.

• •

A TAXI TO THE RESCUE

When I arrived at the train station in Bergen, Norway, at about 10pm, it was absolutely pouring rain, and darker than the inside of a cow. I covered my backpack with a plastic bag, put on my raincoat, and set off grimly toward the local hostel. After fifteen minutes of hard walking I was soaked, as was everything I had with me. After fifteen more minutes I was completely lost. I managed to wade my way back to the train station, where a chap in a Mercedes cab was sitting, dry as a bone in the Sahara, reading a newspaper. Ten minutes later I stepped out of his cab at the hostel. It cost seven dollars. It was money well spent.

• •

Trains

Riding the trains of Europe during the summer puts you squarely in the middle of a giant mass of people on the move. It really can be great fun, and trains are one of the best places to meet people and to exchange information about traveling. I can recall being in a six-person compartment and sharing it with travelers from four different countries. When a young woman claimed the last seat, we asked her where she was from, and she cheerfully replied, "Zimbabwe."

Some train basics follow, and additional information is given in *Basics #2*.

◊ European trains run on military time, that is, the twenty-four clock, so get used to 2pm being written as 1400, 10pm as 2200, and so on. Just subtract twelve and add a "pm" to convert. Also, dates are written in the order of day, month, year. June 12, 1997, would be written numerically as 12-6-97. Be careful with this when entering Flexipass dates. I always write out the month, to avoid confusion.

◊ Many European cities have more than one train station. Paris, for example, has six mainline stations. Make sure that you know where you must leave from, and don't assume that it is the same station that you came into, or even where you may have bought your ticket. Similarly, when planning an arrival, make sure of which station you will be coming into, since some of the others may be a good distance from your intended destination.

◊ When traveling to or from large cities, try to get on your train early, or make a seat reservation. Some trains do fill up, especially in southern Italy, and on weekends and holidays all over Europe, and standing for five hours is never fun. Reservations usually cost a few dollars and can be made when you buy your ticket, or if you have a pass, any time you happen to be at a station. If you know how long you want to stay in a place, making your outbound reservation when you arrive is a good idea.

❖ Reservations are also needed for couchettes, which are bunks for sleeping on night trains. (Sleeping on trains is covered in more detail under "Accommodations," Chapter 8) Night trains leave a city in the evening, and adjust their speed to arrive early the following day, regardless of the distance involved.

❖ There are typically several different kinds of trains in every country. These include high-speed trains such as the AVE and TGV, Eurocities, Intercities, etc – look for the "EC" or "IC" designation in the timetable. Even with a train pass, you can expect to pay a supplement and/or be required to make a reservation on trains like these. This supplement is usually not very much (about $10), especially considering the time saved, but it can be a surprise when you thought the trip would be free. For details on this, see the first page of your free Eurail timetable, or your InterRail bumph.

❖ If you are looking at a long train ride, buy plenty of food and water before heading for the station. Station food is expensive, and train food is even more so.

❖ A yellow stripe over the windows of a car designates first class. Also, always check the door or window of your chosen car for a destination sign. Sometimes trains are split up in mid-journey. Usually, but not always, individual cars will have metal signs near their doors with the car's ultimate destination on them (they don't do this in Britain). Make sure that the car you get into is going to your destination, especially on night trains. Sometimes there are signs on the platforms with diagrams of the train showing which cars are going where. If there are no signs visible anywhere, find a conductor, point to the floor of the car, and state your destination in a questioning tone. They'll let you know if you're in the right car.

❖ The first few pages of the Eurail timetable contain some useful information, including a train user's dictionary in five languages. These few pages are well worth reading. At the back of the timetable there is a list of the standard pictorial symbols used for services in train stations, such as left luggage, lockers, etc.

✧ The free Eurail map has tons of useful information on the back side. This too is well worth reading, and it lists free transportation and discounts you will not find listed anywhere else, as well as pass-abuse penalties. Don't ignore this information.

✧ The same map lists Eurail Aid offices next to the map itself. These offices can issue new maps or timetables and can deal with pass problems. InterRail passholders can use InterRail centers in London, Copenhagen, Oslo and Trondheim, some of which even provide accommodations as well as food and somewhere to get cleaned up.

✧ Once in Europe, under-26s can take advantage of large discounts on a certain type of rail ticket. Known as BIJ tickets, these are available from student and youth travel agencies and can save as much as a third on the price of a regular rail ticket. They're valid for two months and you can stop off wherever you like as long as you keep going in one direction – no backtracking is allowed. These tickets are useful if you want to make one long specific journey and don't need a rail pass.

• •

WHEN IN ROMA . . .

When in the station or using a timetable, remember that some European cities are spelled differently in English than in their native languages. A friend of mine, a professor at UC Berkeley no less, was once astounded to find that no trains went to "Florence." A short list of the most important cities:

Belgrade	Beograd	Lisbon	Lisboa
Brussels	Bruxelles	Milan	Milano
Cologne	Köln	Munich	München
Copenhagen	København	Naples	Napoli
Florence	Firenze	Prague	Praha
Geneva	Genève	Rome	Roma
Genoa	Genova	Turin	Torino
Gothenburg	Göteborg	Venice	Venezia
The Hague	Den Haag	Vienna	Wien

• •

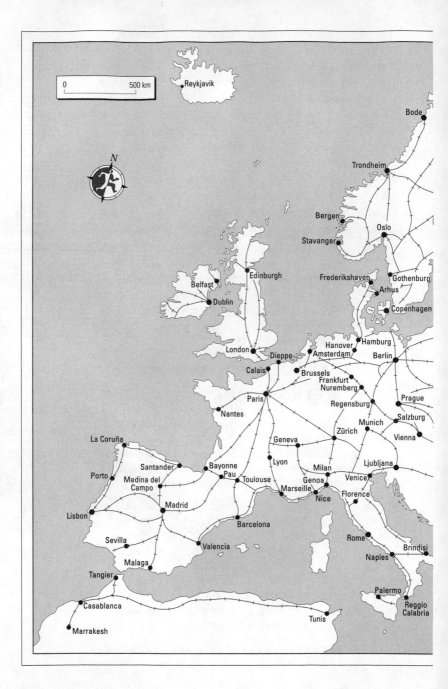

MAJOR
INTERNATIONAL
RAIL ROUTES

Narvik

Rovaniemi

Helsinki

St Petersburg

Stockholm

Tallinn

Riga

Moscow

Vilnius

Gdánsk

Warsaw

Lvov

Budapest

Belgrade

Bucharest

Varna

T'bilisi

Sofia

Istanbul

Ankara

Thessaloniki

Athens

Izmir

Train Stations

One of the nice things about train travel is that a number of travel necessities can be taken care of upon arrival at the train station. Some recommendations:

✧ Virtually every train station in Europe offers some form of luggage storage, either in lockers or at a left-luggage office. These are especially useful for those who bring too much and want to drop off their main pack to live out of a daypack for a while. Old-style lockers have a key, while new lockers print out a combination for you. Be warned that some of the new-style lockers will simply open after the time you have paid for has run out. Make very sure whether or not you have to pay in advance for all the time you use. I prefer the left-luggage office myself, although it may not be open 24 hours. One idea if you happen to remember: When you check a bag, leave a photo ID that you won't need in the bag. That way, if you lose your claim check, you can easily prove that the stuff is yours.

✧ Plan your exit upon arrival. Check the departure times and platforms for the trains going to your next destination. Make a reservation if necessary, or book a couchette if taking a night train. It is very unpleasant to check out of a hostel planning to take a night train and find that there are no more couchettes, or that there is no space altogether.

✧ Buy a phone card if necessary – they're usually available from tobacco or newspaper kiosks. There's more on phone cards in Chapter 11.

✧ Hit the tourist office for maps, the dates of any festivals or events coming up in the local area, and any places in the city to avoid after dark (or altogether).

Train Pass Conservation Strategies

You just paid a lot of money for a Eurail or InterRail pass, and I guarantee that on some of those long train trips you will think long and hard about how to get the most out of it. Here are some ideas, most of which will make more sense after reading *Basics #2*:

- To save some travel days or time on a Eurail Flexipass, or time on an unlimited pass, don't validate your pass until you are ready to really start traveling. For example, if you fly into Madrid, and then intend to go to Pamplona to run with the bulls for a week or so, it is worth buying a ticket (for about $30), rather than starting up your unlimited pass, or starting up and using a day on a Flexipass. Try to plan any long city stays on either end of your trip, for the same reason. If you want to spend two weeks in Paris, don't do it in the middle of your trip while your pass is activated. Balance this, though, with the possible need to take a break mid-trip. If you aren't enjoying your trip because of too much go-go-go, don't keep pushing simply to "get the most" out of a pass.

- Don't forget that even though a Flexipass works off travel days used, it too has a two-month clock ticking, just like an unlimited pass.

- When taking a night train, if you leave after 7pm (1900) you will only be charged one Eurail Flexipass day, for travel up to midnight on the next day (29 hours later). You can cover a lot of ground in 29 hours.

- If you want to make a short to medium-length trip, it may be worth buying a train or bus ticket rather than using a Flexipass day, especially if you are running out of days.

- Remember that England and Scotland are not Eurail or InterRail countries. Go to these places first or last.

- Every May and June sales of erasable pens soar in college bookstores across the nation, as thousands of students prepare to swindle the Flexipass system. Yes, wicked as it may seem, erasing days and changing numbers is rampant among holders of these passes. It happens, and you know it happens, and they know it happens. Officially, conductors should stamp, with a date, every entry you make in your travel day boxes. In reality, they sometimes don't bother, and this opens the door to such originality on the part of pass holders. Fines and penalties are stiff if you are caught; a description of them is included with your pass and is printed on the free map.

❖ Don't let the goal of getting the absolutely, positively last dime out of your pass impact your trip. Above all, don't get so caught up in cheap travel that you skip a trip somewhere interesting just because you might have to buy a train ticket to save a flexi day. You've spent quite a bit of money to get to Europe. Money spent to go places while you're there is usually money well spent.

WARNING: Some of the "free" things offered with your Eurail pass, such as a Rhine cruise, require you to use a day or validate your pass. If something is given free to passholders, it will cost you a validation and/or a day. If something is merely discounted, it will not cost you a day, with the possible exception of the Channel Tunnel (detailed below). Using a Flexipass day to get a "free" boat ride that would only cost fifteen dollars to buy outright is a waste. Thanks and a tip of the hat to Brian at the Forsyth Travel Library for this information.

Ferries and the Channel Tunnel

Two ferry crossings that many travelers will make are the English Channel and the infamous Brindisi to Patras crossing to Greece, which can be similar to the trip described in Chapter 2. This is, incidentally, "free" to holders of the right InterRail pass.

Apart from the Channel ferries and those between Italy and Greece, others that you might want to consider are those between France and Ireland, which are "free" with a Eurail pass. Your Eurail map will show discounted and "free" ferry routes, as will your InterRail information.

"Free" ferry lines will almost always have some way of squeezing money out of you, however. "Summer supplements" and port or departure taxes are common tactics. Don't be surprised if your "free" trip ends up costing you twenty or thirty dollars and a Flexipass day. This is especially true on the Italy to Greece run.

When taking an overnight ferry, you will usually have several price-dependent seating choices. The cheapest option is "deck," which allows you to find a place on deck or on a bench to camp out. Most ferries also offer airline-type seats for a bit more, but expect clouds of smoke. A bunk in a cabin is the most expensive option, but even that can be cheap enough to fit into a very tight budget. You don't have to pay for the whole room – bunks are usually sold individually. That ten bucks you could save by sleeping on deck (an experience described in Chapter 2) may not be worth it.

Ferry food is very expensive and rarely appealing: Bring enough food and water to last the journey. Coins from all countries served are accepted on almost all ferries. Finally, when you get on a ferry, think of the time zone change. Crossing the English Channel, crossing from Italy to Greece, and crossing from Sweden to Finland each involve a one-hour shift.

Channel Crossings

The Channel is crisscrossed by hundreds of ferries, hovercraft, jetfoils, and other craft, and there are dozens of ways to get from England to the rest of Europe. The shortest crossing, not surprisingly, is at the closest point between France and England (Dover to Calais) and some Eurailers opt for this. Others choose similar trips from one of the nearby ports such as Oostende in Belgium, on which there is a Eurail discount, or Boulogne. There are 50 percent discounts on many Channel crossings for InterRail under-26 pass holders, although those with the 26+ pass will find the selection much less extensive. Most of the vessels crossing the Channel are car and passenger ferries, although some routes are covered by hovercraft and jetfoils. These make the trip across the Channel in less than half the time of a ferry, but you can't get out on deck and walk around. Some things to remember about crossing the Channel:

❖ Since England is not a Eurail country, you will have to pay for your rail ticket between London and the port in Britain (about $35 from London to Dover, for example). You also have to pay with an InterRail pass, although discounts are available.

❖ Even though the boats are slower, they do allow you to get a beautiful view of the white cliffs of Dover when approaching or leaving England. You can't get this on the jetfoil, and the cliffs really are worth seeing at least once.

❖ Money-changing facilities on the ferry or at the port will cost you your eyeteeth, so change money before leaving for the ferry. Traveling to Britain from the continent, you should remember this because you'll need money to buy an onward ticket to London when you arrive. Or you could buy this ticket at wherever you're setting out from, although this may cost a small amount extra.

❖ There is a decent (35 percent) Eurail discount on ferries and jetfoils from Oostende to Ramsgate and Dover, with the jetfoil service costing slightly more. InterRail passes usually give 50 percent, and on a wider variety of routes.

❖ Since England is still not a Eurail country, your Eurail timetable lists the channel port city rather than London as the destination. For example, if you're traveling to London from Paris using the boats and jetfoils that operate out of Oostende, look up "Oostende" as the destination to reach from Paris. Then check the Oostende ferry schedule (also in your timetable) to see if there will be a ferry or jetfoil to meet your train from Paris. The ferry/jetfoil and train terminal in Oostende are one and the same, and for some trains from Paris there is only a ten-minute wait for a departure to England. Typically, trains will also meet ferries and other crafts on both sides of the Channel, but check before you choose your ferry, in case there is a lengthy wait.

❖ British readers finally face a challenge at this point: finding the best combination of ferry and/or land transportation to get from their homes to the continent. Call a travel agent for information on when and where ferries leave your area, then prepare to juggle prices, discounts, arrival times, etc. Compare your best options with the expense of traveling to Ramsgate or Dover and leaving from there. Don't expect companies to give a full range of options – most will claim never to have even heard of their competitors. Also consider the availability of onward transport from your ferry's destination. A cheap ferry into an industrial port miles from the nearest train station won't seem like such a good deal after a long walk or taxi ride.

❖ When ferrying out of England, don't just think France. Ferries also go to Norway, Sweden, Germany, the Netherlands, and Spain. If your main destination is Scandinavia, consider one long ferry trip straight there rather than a short ferry ride to, say, Calais, followed by a long train journey. It's competitive both in price and travel time. And, again, there are good discounts for holders of InterRail passes.

❖ Watch out for the one-hour time change.

The Channel Tunnel

The Channel Tunnel is now open for business, offering three-hour trips between London and Paris, and a three-and-a-quarter-hour service between London and Brussels. About ten Eurostar trains per day run between London and Paris, and four per day between London and Brussels. Any type of seventeen-country Eurail pass, a Europass that includes France, or a France RailPass will give you a discount. A Britrail pass will not unless purchased directly from British Rail. The current second-class one-way price, which may go up or down depending on traffic volume through the tunnel, is $95 with a Eurail pass – a 30 percent discount on the full advance purchase fare of around $140. Using a pass for this discount does not cost you a travel day. It may or may not activate your pass – the Eurostar folks are a bit haphazard in enforcing their activation requirements. A regular train from Paris to London will cost a pass-holder about seventy dollars and a train pass travel day, and it takes about eight hours, making the tunnel a good idea even for pass users. For those on two- or three-week trips, it is definitely worth the price to save a day in Paris or London. Again, full details in *Basics #2*.

●●

FLYING WITHIN EUROPE

Greece is a very common destination for first-time travelers in Europe. Consider the following example for a situation when flying makes sense. Let's say you are in London, and want to go to Ios and drink yourself into a hospital bed. Ios is good for that. With a Eurail pass you would pay to cross the Channel (Eurail is not valid in England) by either Channel Tunnel train, ferry and train, bus, or whatever. You would then proceed, probably via Paris, to Rome, and on to the hellhole port of Brindisi, to catch a ferry to Athens. The train ride from Paris to Brindisi will take roughly eighteen hours. You then get on the ferry in Brindisi, pay a port tax and summer supplement (even with a ferry that takes Eurail passes), and then spend the night sleeping either on the deck or in a room full of smoke. The next morning you arrive in Patras on the west coast of Greece, and pay for a bus, or wait for a train, to Piraeus, the port of Athens, which will probably involve a transfer. At the port you pay full price for a ferry, and spend another night on deck on the way to Ios, where you arrive the next morning.

Sounds great, doesn't it? I've done it and it stinks. It's less painful if you start from Rome, but it's still eight hours from Rome to Brindisi. And you have to do the whole process in reverse to get back. The total cost, including couchettes, port taxes, etc, is around $120. Flying out of London to Athens, on the other hand, will cost about two hundred dollars round trip, and you will arrive feeling like a human being instead of a piece of raw meat. The cost of flying is about eighty dollars more than the cost of taking the train, but you avoid five days of almost constant and very unpleasant travel. Also, if you've got a Eurail flexipass, you save a whopping five travel days, at a cost of roughly forty dollars per day. With an unlimited pass, flying saves you time and misery. With a flexipass, it saves you time, misery, and big, big bucks. Even better, if you can get a flight from London directly to one of the larger islands, rather than to Athens, you don't need to think about the cost and hassle of the ferry. The pleasure of sitting on a beach sipping a beer while others are cursing their lives in Brindisi is worth it. And when you're ready to leave, you get on the plane and you get off a few hours later in London.

Other than Greece, the really incredible deals out of London are to Turkey, Egypt, and Israel – and to some extent to Spain and Portugal, too. Check and see what deals are available when you arrive in London, and plan ahead if you are coming back and can take advantage of something. Also, no matter how you get to one of these exotic locales, you may be able to get a cheap charter back to London. Don't count on this, though, if you have to catch a flight home on the day after your charter is due to arrive. Charter companies vary in their reliability and may leave you in the lurch.

• •

Creative Transportation

If your train pass has run out or if you want to conserve one, or you never had one, you might want to consider one of the following ways of getting around.

Ride-Sharing

Ride-sharing is highly recommended if you have more time than money, and is always worth an inquiry, unless you have an unlimited Eurail pass. It's sort of an organized hitchhiking service, whereby drivers with extra room offer seats for sale through an agency. The agency then tries to match the empty seats with travelers going to the drivers' destinations. Most European countries have one or more of these agencies. As an example, Munich to Hamburg cost me 63 marks in total – dirt cheap compared with a train or bus ticket. The big disadvantage of this mode of travel is the uncertainty of finding someone going both where you want to go and when you want to go there. However, for someone who has no fixed schedule, who is happy to wander all over Europe wherever the next driver takes him, or someone who is trying to conserve Flexipass days, this way of getting around is fantastic. I suppose other disadvantages could include being stuck for hours in a car with a cigar-smoking loudmouth possessed of a five-gallon bladder, but that hasn't happened to me yet. Also, even though ride-sharing is much safer than hitchhiking for women, if you are female and are uncomfortable getting into a car with a particular person, don't accept the ride. Or, you can ask only for rides from women, to be on the ultra-safe side. Enquire about ride-sharing services at tourist offices and hostels. Big cities are good, and big cities with universities are better. If you are near a university, you could always check out the college notice-boards. Otherwise, consult the list below, which is by no means comprehensive but covers the major national services I've been able to find.

RIDE-SHARE SERVICES

1. Austria (Vienna) - Mitzfahrzentrale 0222-587-4225
2. Belgium (Brussels) - Taxi Stop 02-646-8610
3. France (Paris) - Allostop 42-26-00-66
4. Germany (most cities) - Mitzfahrzentrale 19-444
5. Britain (Newcastle) - Freewheelers 0191-222-0090
6. Holland (Amsterdam) - Intl. Lift Center 020-622-4342
7. Switzerland (Zurich) - Mitzfahrzentrale 261-6893

Hitchhiking

I've done it, but I don't recommend it, for obvious reasons. I once met a five foot, ninety pound, sixteen-year-old Polish girl who had hitchhiked, from Warsaw to Rome, alone. When she told me that I actually felt my skin crawl. If you do wish to hitch, remember that Europe is somewhat safer than the States, but not totally safe by any means. Women should not hitchhike alone. Period. Some tips for those who insist on hitching:

♦ Using a sign, especially for women, can be dangerous. Don't use one, and when someone stops, ask where *they* are going. That way the driver cannot lie about his destination to get you into his car.

♦ If at all possible, keep your luggage with you, and pull it out of the back seat before getting out of the car. If you put it in the trunk, you may get out at your destination only to watch your backpack disappear down the road in a squeal of tires. The same thing goes for gas and bathroom stops.

♦ Some hitchhikers use a flag to appeal to their traveling compatriots. I suggest bringing your state flag, as people may stop out of curiosity.

♦ Most student-oriented guidebooks usually have a few sentences on where to hitch out of major cities.

♦ Women who hitch will have rapid success in groups of three or less. Men in groups of one or more will be waiting a long time.

♦ Finally, if you are hitching, be very, very careful. If it feels wrong, it probably is wrong. A long walk or a bed for the night is better than a ride that ends up in robbery or worse.

I SHOULDA' GONE BY TRAIN

Once, when hitching in Italy, I had spent an entire morning baking in the sun and sucking exhaust fumes. At first, I found relief in profanity. When that failed me, I used blasphemy. As I stood there, a young woman came out of a nearby store, and began walking toward the road. Before she even got to the shoulder a Mercedes slammed on its brakes and pulled over in front of her. Without breaking stride she pulled the door open. She then asked a few questions, jumped in the front seat, and roared off, leaving me standing there. Such is the lot of the male hitchhiker.

Buses

If you do not have a rail pass, and need to get to a specific destination at a specific time, then buses are hard to beat for a cheap ride. Unfortunately, buses are also hard to beat for inflicting pain, and few experiences are as agonizing as a long or overnight ride on a crowded bus. Basically, you're paying for the low price with discomfort. This discomfort is somewhat mitigated if you are comfortable enough with your seat partner to sleep sprawled all over each other. I recommend buses if you have the specific time/place/need mentioned, and especially if the alternative is a long, expensive train ride. I once took a bus from Copenhagen to London. Yes, I was a pitiful, whimpering wreck by the end of the nineteen-hour trip, but it saved about $120 over a train ticket. For that kind of money, I can be miserable for one night.

CHAPTER EIGHT

ACCOMMODATIONS

Most travelers automatically think of hostels when they think of budget accommodations. Hostels usually are the cheapest and best way to go if you're on a tight budget, but there are exceptions, especially if you are traveling in a couple or a group. Two or more people can often find a room in a hotel or pension for about the same price as an equivalent number of hostel beds, and often with much better amenities. So, especially if you are in a group, don't simply march to the nearest hostel and ignore all other possibilities. Shopping around can save you time, keep you away from packed and noisy dorms, and maybe even save you money. This is where Commandments One, Two, and Three rear their happy heads in triplicate. If you are traveling light, it's much easier to spend some time going around to several places before choosing one. If you've arrived early, you have more options than someone who shows up as night is falling. And if you've planned ahead, you have a reservation somewhere, so you're not searching out of desperation.

One handy tip, which I will try and repeat elsewhere: Europeans like to travel too. Since they can get to major tourist attractions and major cities on weekends, they do this a lot. (At Neuschwanstein Castle in Bavaria, the most touristy of places, at least two-thirds of the crowd on the day I went chose the tour given in German.) Try and time your arrival at major cities, and your visits to major attractions, for days other than Friday, Saturday, and holidays.

In general, the price of accommodations declines as you move south and east. Don't go only to hostels in Portugal, Spain, Greece, and especially in Eastern Europe. In Scandinavia, on the other hand, hostels and camping are usually the only accommodations that are even remotely affordable, especially for solo travelers. In other countries, the size of the city may make the difference. For example, a hostel in a village in England I once went to charged £12 for breakfast and a bed in a very large, but very clean, dorm. In the same town, a beautiful little bed and breakfast charged £13 for a single room that looked like something out of *House and Garden*. The sweet old woman who owned the place made me sandwiches when I showed up after the local pub had closed, and proudly showed me pictures of her son, the Police Constable. It was worth the extra "quid", believe me.

The Accommodation Hunt

If you do not have a room reservation when you arrive, prepare to play "Who's got a room?" No matter how you arrive in a city, even with your own transport, use the phone to search for a place, either out of your guidebook or from a tourist office. Using the tourist office can make your bed-hunting easier: They should have the latest information on local accommodation, and can often make a booking for you (they may charge a fee for this). If they can't call for you, get a phone card and call around before heading out to look at places. Obvious? Of course. But you'd be surprised how many fall into the temptation of "This one's only five minutes away – let's just go there." Also, don't quit calling if the first place has beds. Either way, if it's a pit when you get there, you'll have to hike back to the station and start over. Find two or three places with rooms, start with the one that sounded best, friendliest, cheapest, whatever you want, and go take a look.

When you arrive, ask a few questions. (1) Always ask to see the room *you* will be renting. Consider how noisy it will be at night. (2) Always ask how much the room will cost in total, with all taxes, fees, charges for breakfast, and the like included, to avoid nasty surprises when you check out. (3) Take a good look at your fellow lodgers. A bunch of men with pencil-thin mustaches picking their teeth with stilettos is usually a bad sign. (4) If possible, ask someone staying there if they like it and if there is anything you should know. (5) Owners and staff may not show you the cheapest room first. If that is important to you, ask up front for the cheapest available, and then work up in price if you don't like it. (6) If you ask for a room and the person behind the desk asks how long you will be staying, "three days" is probably the answer they're looking for. If you're staying longer than three days, especially if the place isn't crowded, ask for a discount. You may get it. (7) If you are alone, and only doubles are available, ask if you can share with a single person who comes later. Or you may have to find a roommate yourself if you really want/need that room. Note that all these points imply that you have a choice of going somewhere else. If every place is packed except the one you're at, however, your choice will be easy.

If there is no tourist office in your town and nothing about that town in your guidebook, you're probably well off the beaten track. Good for you. To look for housing, ask some of the station staff if they know of a cheap place to stay. Taxi drivers are also potential sources of information, although they may not offer anything which does not involve a taxi ride. Hotels tend to cluster around train stations: even if they are out of your price range (and they may not be – station areas are often home to the cheapest places), they may be able to direct you somewhere else.

If the first place you go to is full, don't panic. First off, ask the owner/staff of the place that's full if they know of any place that isn't; you can be sure that he knows his local competition. Also ask if you can call from there, and potentially save yourself a long walk. If the owner can't help you at all, or if everything is full, return to the train station and start the whole process over. (This is when you will be blessing your light backpacks, and swearing to call me and thank me for harping on the idea of going light. You will forget as soon as you find a bed, but that's only human.) You may have to adjust the maximum amount you're willing to pay if things get really bad.

In a large city, one option to consider before paying a lot more is "commuting": staying outside of that city and traveling in by train each day. The accommodations you find in a suburb or small town will probably be cheaper, nicer and less crowded than in the city center, and the money you save will probably offset the cost of the commute, especially if you have an unlimited rail pass that you can use for the daily round trip. If you're hosteling, you may find yourself doing this anyway, as hostels are often situated outside of city centers.

In a city or a small town, if it really looks as if you may not find any accommodation at all, and you can't commute, before you spend another five hours looking, give yourself an out. Check the train schedules. Find one going to a place listed in your guidebook. Call ahead to make a reservation. At least that way there is a bed somewhere with your name on it. If your search for a bed does come up empty, you can always get on a train and go to your reservation. And if all else fails, you can always catch a night train, with or without couchette.

Please be reassured that situations like this are rare, except in cases of very late arrival in major cities or tourist centers, or if there is a major event taking place in the area. In almost every case spending more money will guarantee finding a room. Rooms in the nicer hotels in a town will still be available long after all hostel and budget rooms in a city have sold out.

AGENTS AND "TOUTS"

When you arrive at train stations, especially if you are wearing a backpack, you may be approached by a bed agent or "tout" who tries to sell you on staying at his or her hostel or hotel. These people are rarely criminals, but they can represent all levels of accommodation, from the vile and bug-infested to the surprisingly nice. (Bugs outnumber surprises by about ten to one.) Most of the time they represent places the guidebooks have passed over, either accidentally or for a reason. Single women should be careful with these guys, just in case. Other travelers may want to give these places a look, but only after first grilling the tout (on the spot) about every aspect of the place. How much does it cost? How many beds per room? What floor of the building is it on? Are there lockers or a guarded luggage room? Is there a lock-out during the day for cleaning? Is there a curfew? How close is it to the metro/bus/tram stop? Is someone at the front desk all night? Can we get a room together? Are the dorms coed? How many beds per room was that again? Are there laundry facilities? And the one question that's sure to bring forth a lie: "How far is it from here?" "Five minutes" is the universal answer to that question – if you get there in ten, you're doing well. If you decide to go and look, when you get there, ask to see the room *you* will be staying in, take a long look at the bathrooms, and give the rest of the place the once-over. If it looks good, then consider it. If you decide to stay, cancel any other reservations you may have made, but only for the next few days, in case you want to move. In the Greek Islands, touts will usually meet you at the boat, and will sometimes be aggressive – though they'll just as often be sweet little old ladies with a room to let. If they *don't* meet you, you've got a problem. Start looking hard.

In Eastern Europe, especially Prague, the "tout" may also be a grandmother offering a bed in her apartment. These are often a good deal, and can offer a glimpse into the realities of life after forty years of the Communist paradise. Ask the same questions before going to have a look, but don't give some nice old woman the third degree.

Hostels

Since you will probably be spending a large amount of your time staying in hostels, I think they are worth a fairly long look. Starting at the beginning: Hostels are shared accommodation, usually sex-segregated, consisting of five to ten to forty beds per room or dormitory. Bathroom facilities are also shared. Usually there are some smaller rooms for families or couples, but these fill up fast. The actual building housing all of these beds can vary from spartan to highly elaborate: Some hostels are little more than barracks, whereas others are in castles, beautiful old houses, or rustic farm buildings. Facilities you can expect in most hostels are luggage storage, lockers, a kitchen for those cooking for themselves, some kind of common room and usually laundry facilities. Many places serve breakfast, and some, not many, serve dinner. Most, I would guess two out of three, close from roughly October 1 until May 15, depending on local conditions.

The majority of hostels are part of the long-established Hosteling International group (formerly the International Youth Hostels Association), and their affiliated hostels are normally of a high standard – very clean, very well equipped, and in large cities, often very full. However, with the boom in budget travel more and more "private" hostels have opened, particularly in larger cities, and these can be as basic or as elaborate or as clean or as dirty as the owner chooses.

Other than always choosing an HI-affiliated hostel, there is no way to predict what your hostel will be like with certainty, especially since the other people staying there, especially in your room, will be a large part of your hostel experience. Your guidebook might have some information. In general, though, the older, smaller, and more isolated the hostel is, the better. Small towns are better than big cities, and the attitude of the hostel staff can make a huge difference. Having said that, one of the best nights of my life was spent in a large, full, private hostel in the center of Rome, which had a staff that genuinely hated humanity. The people who were staying there with me made all the difference, as did my willingness to get out and meet them. The hostel was terrible, the people were great.

Modern Hostels

Back in the Dark Ages, hostels were different from today. They were exclusively for the young, they closed during the day, there was a curfew at night, every guest was assigned chores, and supposedly more than a few were run like prisons by power-crazed wardens. I tell you this because any or all of these quaint features may still be present at the hostel you stay in. Chores have pretty much gone the way of the dodo, as have age restrictions. Some, I would guess maybe half of all hostels, impose some kind of lock-out so they can clean the place – usually from 10am to 3pm – but late-night curfews are getting few and far between, which can be unfortunate, as one drunk can wake up forty other people. Finally, I have yet to meet the proverbial "Attila the Warden."

●●

OLDER HOSTELERS

The term "Youth Hostel" has probably discouraged millions of somewhat older people from staying in hostels or from taking trips altogether because of the high cost of accommodations. However, except in Bavaria (where you must be 26 or under), there are no age restrictions in official HI hostels (which is partly why they were renamed), and I can't imagine any private hostels imposing them unless they were full. "Youth" may have priority in some other places, but during several months of traipsing around Europe at the advanced age of 31, and staying, for the most part, in hostels, I was never turned away because of my age. In fact, there were a number of times when I was the youngest person staying in a hostel, and once when I was the only one in the place below fifty. While the clientele of most hostels does tend toward the young and the restless, you will find plenty of older travelers, especially Europeans, hosteling away happily into their sixties and or seventies. Don't let the feeling that you may be "too old" stop you from traveling or staying in hostels. Uncouth youths who do not respect their elders can usually be silenced by reminiscing about seeing Jimi Hendrix or Jim Morrison live in concert, whether you did or not.

● ●

Prices and reservations

Since all you are paying for in a hostel is a bed and the use of common facilities, they can be very cheap – I've paid as little as six dollars. In major cities, however, they can cost quite a bit – $26 was the most I've ever paid, although that was in central London. Other cities will fall between those figures, usually in the $14–20 range – dirt cheap compared with a hotel, but not as cheap as you'd like, I'm sure. As we will see in the section on pensions, a hostel may be the cheapest in terms of dollars per bed, but not have the privacy and quiet of a pension or a B+B. Also, crime in hostels does occur, but usually to the unwary or unwise.

Since hostels are the accommodation of choice for most budget travelers, they can fill up quickly, especially in the summer, especially on weekends, and roughly in order of how they're listed in *Let's Go*. If you are planning on staying in a hostel in a major city during June, July, or August, especially in an HI hostel, you must call ahead or risk a long hot walk followed by a longer, hotter walk back. Before I got to that place in Rome, I had metroed, bussed, and walked all the way out to the Ostello de Foro Italico, and waited an hour for the place to open (at the end of a one-hundred person line). I never even saw the reception desk before they filled up. I should have called ahead. Maybe two weeks ahead.

One way to avoid this situation is to book a room from one hostel to another. Many HI hostels will call ahead for you, take a one-night deposit, and give you a receipt to take to your next place. Other hostels will call ahead to other places for you, especially if the two places are owned by the same person. Always ask other travelers for their recommendations, and if you can't get the numbers of the places they recommend, ask your hostel's staff for help in calling information or in making the calls. Finally, don't forget the HI hostel guidebook and map mentioned in Chapter 4 – these are essential if you are going to be hosteling a lot.

••

HI MEMBERSHIP

If you're going to be staying at even a few HI-affiliated hostels anywhere in Europe, you'll need to join. This costs $25 a year if you are between 18 and 55, and $15 if you are under 17 or over 55. They're available from student travel offices, the American Youth Hostels Association direct at PO Box 37613, Washington, DC 20013 (✆202-783-6161), or from around forty local HI offices all over the US and Canada – check the business section of your local phone book. Also, the Forsyth Travel Library sells memberships and will ship your card in a hurry. See *Basics* #1 for their number. Finally, as procrastinators will be happy to hear, you can always join at your first hostel.

••

Hotels

Inexpensive hotels can be found in Europe that are livable and even nice, so don't think that "cheap" automatically means dirty or sleazy. For couples, or anyone who is sick of the hostel scene, there are small, cheap hotels out there that are clean and comfortable, if a bit basic. If you can handle a bathroom down the hall, you increase your choices tremendously. There are, of course, plenty of miserable roach ranches as well, so you may have to do some looking before finding something that matches your budget and standards.

Hotels that cost about the same may vary drastically in terms of cleanliness, comfort, and other amenities. It mostly depends on the owner's attitude. A ten-room hotel that has been run by the same family for two hundred years may lack modern plumbing or central heating, but I'd much rather stay there than at a new two-hundred-room hotel with an absentee owner and a lackadaisical staff. Be aware that traditional European hotels will almost always be cheaper and have more "atmosphere" than those that have been built to "American" standards and designed for tourists.

In Eastern Europe, or somewhere like Turkey, where hostels may be a bit dingy, even a single traveler can afford a hotel, while groups of two or more are good to go. The local hostel will obviously be cheaper, but not always by that much; and the question is really what you are willing to live with – or in. It's usually worth checking the hostel first, as you may get lucky. If it looks bad, move on up the ladder until your money and amenity standards converge.

Pensions

The distinction between a hotel and a pension is a blurry one. In my mind, a pension is run by an owner who lives on-site, and the building wasn't necessarily built to accommodate paying guests. The facilities are usually a bit more extensive than in a bed and breakfast (see the next section), and include things like a common room where the guests can sit and eat together, things that make the place "homier" than a hotel. Like the perfect bed and breakfast (run by the apple-cheeked woman who treats you like family), the perfect pension – full of colorful locals, run by a jovial man named Luigi who makes great pasta – is the Holy Grail of budget travel: much sought-after, rarely found. By definition, these places are almost never in guidebooks; otherwise, they would long ago have been swamped with travelers. When travelers do find places like this, they guard their names and locations as if they were state secrets. The atmosphere in a pension depends greatly on the attitude and personality of the owner. Some of these places fit the dream, others are clip joints full of creepy-crawlies with both two and six legs. In Italy, especially in rural areas, and in France, Spain, and Portugal – somewhere out there that perfect pension exists. But you won't find it in a guidebook.

Bed and Breakfasts

There are more bed and breakfasts in Britain and Ireland than you can imagine – they're everywhere. Unlike the States and Canada, where B+Bs have certain snob appeal and can cost a fortune, the $25 B+B is alive and well in rural Britain. This can make rural travel very pleasant: Since there are so many B+Bs available, you can blissfully ignore the rule of planning ahead during the week. Wander at will until the right place strikes you, settle there for a day or two, get a recommendation on a place in the next town or valley, and move on.

In small towns, in Britain and elsewhere, B+Bs are almost all sidelines: people in houses designed for large families with room to spare. They can be a bit more elaborate in larger cities, and there is an unfortunate tendency for ugly little bathrooms to be jammed into bedrooms to satisfy those too shy to walk down a hallway to the shower, or for extra "stars" in their official ratings. B+Bs are generally more expensive than hostels in cities, closer in price even a few miles away from the tourist hordes, and very competitive in the country, as previously mentioned. Try a rural B+B at least once on your trip if you can.

In other countries, the B+B/pension distinction, as detailed earlier, is not so obvious, nor are there so many per square meter.

Camping

I arbitrarily divide campers into two broad categories: those who are going for a backwoods/wilderness experience, and those who are camping in order to see the cities and countryside of Europe as cheaply as possible. Camping is the cheapest form of accommodation in Europe, but be warned: It is much more enjoyable if you are traveling by car. Taking a train to a city and then carrying all of the normal budget traveler load, plus tent, stove, real sleeping bag, and other camping essentials out to a campsite is often a daunting prospect. Consider this if you plan to use camping as your primary means of accommodation.

Before you plan on camping your way across Europe, think about how much you would enjoy living out of a tent for two months while camping at home. Camping in Europe is a bit more settled than in other continents, and campgrounds are generally well equipped with amenities, especially in France – a nation of campers. Nevertheless, sixty days in a tent is a long time. If you plan this, try and budget for at least a few nights in a bed. Tips follow for the tenting crowd:

❖ For the ultra, ultra budgeters, hitching rides from campground to campground with Europeans on vacations is sometimes possible, especially if you assure your ride that you won't ask for another one at the next campground.

✧ One very important piece of advice: Expect and plan for rain. For backwoods types, even though you're not in the Rockies or the Sierras, don't underestimate British, and especially Scottish, weather. A change of a few hundred feet in altitude, or a very few minutes, can bring a total change in weather, from sun to blowing, chilly rain. Triple this warning in Scandinavia and in the former Soviet Union.

✧ Bring a good stove, as very few organized campgrounds allow fires. As mentioned in the "What to Bring" Section, "Gaz" stoves are the standard unit all over Europe.

✧ Norway and Sweden allow "free camping," a great institution. Under the law, you have the right to camp anywhere on public or private land as long as you stay no longer than two days, clean up after yourself, and are not within 150 meters of any buildings. This can be a low-cost lifesaver in these expensive countries. In other countries, a polite inquiry to the local landowner may get you a low-impact, no-fire campsite.

✧ An International Camping Carnet, which is similar to a hostel membership card, is required at a few campgrounds and ignored in many others. For thirty dollars, you may get a discount, priority if the place is full, and, most important, you don't have to leave your passport with the campground office. They are available from *Family Campers*, 4804 Transit Road, Building 2, Depew, NY 14043.

✧ Good books on camping in Europe are few and far between in North America. Dedicated campers might want to get a copy of *Europa Camping and Caravanning*, available from Recreational Equipment, Inc, which is listed in *Basics #7*.

Mooching off Friends and Acquaintances

Now here is the ideal accommodation if you can find it. Trading addresses and invitations is very common among travelers in Europe, and it may be worth changing your plans to accept an invitation. You will probably end up well off the tourist trail and get a glimpse into the real everyday life of your host's country. If you do accept such hospitality, remember that your hosts will probably be working or going to school and may not have the time to show you around. Plan to arrive on a weekend. It is also a nice gesture to spend some of the money you'll save on accommodation to take your friend(s) out, bring a gift when you arrive, or buy a truckload of beer and throw a party that destroys their apartment. It is considered bad form to be given an invitation and then arrive in town six weeks later and expect to be welcomed immediately. A postcard or phone call in the interim to alert your future hosts as to your intentions is both smart and polite.

Other Accommodations

Other accommodations are as varied as the imagination: YMCAs, YWCAs, monasteries and convents in Italy (not much partying there), private homes – whatever turns up if you look beyond the guidebook. Even though you will probably be hosteling a lot, I do recommend trying out other options; you may be pleasantly surprised. Your local tourist office is a good start, and don't be shy about asking other travelers about unusual places they have stayed.

One possibility to consider, especially if you want a single room and some peace and quiet, is student housing. These are university residence halls that are opened to travelers when school is out for the summer. Rooms are usually quite small, simple, and clean. Worth looking into, especially for a couple, or for a hostel break. As a bonus, you can talk to your friends about "your time spent at the London School of Economics." These are usually listed in guidebooks, but you should also check at the tourist office if you're interested.

STUDENT HOUSING IN PRAGUE

The unquestioned king of student housing opportunities has to be in Prague, where a simply enormous complex of dormitories is partially open for business every summer. This is Communist architecture at its finest: concrete slabs and plenty of 'em. Scattered throughout this rabbit warren of about twelve high-rise dormitories are tiny bars, pubs, discos, stores, restaurants, and other facilities, all with incredibly cheap prices. Beer in the pub is cheaper per liter than soda from the stores. Two dollars, at least in 1996, bought lunch for two from one of those stores.

This complex is also good for a glimpse at how students lived under the old system of government. Amid these bleak, depressing buildings it is still possible to get a tiny feel for what life was like before the "Velvet Revolution" of 1989 brought freedom to what was then Czechoslovakia.

Sleep-Inns and Slum Hostels

This is one accommodation option that you may only want to try if everything else is unavailable. Genuine sleep-inns, at least in my experience, open only in the summers, and are mainly there to keep people from sleeping on the streets when the local hostels are overrun (Amsterdam's "Sleep-In" is an exception and is open year-round). They are aptly named, since there is little to do but sleep in one of these places, and a bed is pretty much all they provide. Expect huge, crowded dorms full to the rafters. Imagine two doors, one saying "Beds 1–75," and the other "Beds 76–150." That's when you pray for the ghost of John Wesley Hardin to make an appearance, and with plenty of ammunition. These places are better than nothing, but are not real hostels; and sometimes they're not even much of a cost-saver. For example, in Copenhagen, the Amager hostel has only two- and five-bed rooms, and charges 108 crowns (about $20) for breakfast and a bed in a five-bed room. It has a kitchen, laundry, playground, TV room, serves a hot dinner, and so on. The "City Public

Hostel," actually a sleep-inn, has the two dorms just mentioned, and a few smaller rooms, and charges 115 crowns, with breakfast. The point is not that sleep-inns are run by bad people; they fill a need as best they can. However, if you end up in one of these places, get out as soon as possible. Don't make the mistake of thinking that all hostels are like this or that once in a place like this, you're stuck.

The same goes for some of the private "hostels" that appear like mushrooms after rain all over congested summertime Europe – slum hostels, basically. Imagine paying 28 German marks (about $18) to sleep in a basement, with forty other people in one room, on dirty mattresses that are either on the floor or thrown on pallets. I don't have to imagine, because I've done it, and every single one of the other beds was full, so a lot of other people have, too. No facilities whatsoever, just a mattress and a bathroom.

These places are opened up, often temporarily, by greedy people who see a need and want to fill it as cheaply and profitably as possible. Their natural prey are those who wait until they arrive in town to find accommodations, and especially those who arrive late in the day, tired, loaded with stuff, and willing to take anything just to end the housing search and keep from sleeping in the train station that night. As I have said before, if you are going to a major city, especially in July or August, plan ahead, and you may avoid having to join them.

Sleeping on Trains

Sleeping on trains, surprisingly, does not save money so much as time. Especially on a short trip, wasted days sitting in a train are frustrating, and some people recommend traveling almost entirely by night train so the days can be spent sightseeing. If you could get a decent night's sleep, this might be true, but the various noises, stops, border crossings, and other disturbances that occur on any train journey mean this can be difficult for all but the heaviest sleepers. Bear in mind, also, that taking night trains cuts down on some of the best times to see Europe: mornings, and especially at night, when most cities come alive. That said, a night train here and there can be a sensible use of limited time. If you want to sleep on a train, on a budget at least, you have three options: a seat, a reclining seat in a compartment, or a couchette. There are also "hotel trains" and sleepers in first class, but you could charter a plane for the cost of one of those beds.

Sleeping in an upright seat is recommended only if you are Catholic and doing a penance – and you must have done something pretty bad to deserve this. Reclining seats are better, especially if you are in a group, and especially if your group has the compartment to itself. However, whether or not you get a train with reclining seats is a matter of luck and simply depends on how the train happens to be constructed. They very rarely cost any extra. Note that the six seats in a compartment usually convert into only three "beds" (the bottom part of the seat pulls out, while the backrest can be pushed down), and you then have a choice of either sleeping foot to head to foot, and smelling feet all night, or head to head to head, and waking up with a person who mistakes you for their spouse or sweetie. Note also that if the train is half full or less, everyone can stretch out, and if it's completely full, nobody can. It is therefore worth your while to get in an empty compartment as early as you can, and then to look as unsavory as possible in the hope of warding off people. Groups of three or more should try to reserve seats in a single compartment for the same reason.

If you're prepared to pay a little extra, couchettes are, in my opinion, the way to go. Couchettes are benches that convert to separate bunks and are grouped four or six per compartment. If you're in a large enough group, by all means try to get a compartment to yourselves and whoop it up. Sheets are supplied, and there is a total charge of about eighteen dollars for bunk and linen, whether or not you have a train pass. They are sold without regard to age, sex, or marital status, and I truly believe the reservation agents delight in mixing strange groups together. When you are making a couchette reservation (and you should do so as soon as you know when you're leaving), ask for an upper bunk. These are quieter and a bit less liable to theft, and you don't have people climbing past you at odd hours.

Sleeping out, or in Train Stations

Before you do either of these, think long and hard about spending more money than normal, or catching a train somewhere else. Sleeping in stations used to be quite popular with penniless student travelers, but it is now less so. It is safer than sleeping in a park, especially if someone in a group stays up to keep an eye on things, but a train station at 3:30am does not attract the most lovable characters. You may be asked by security to show a ticket at some stations these days, especially if you look a bit

"alternative." Setting up shop near some business that will stay open all night, or near the security office itself if possible, is a good idea.

Sleeping out – in parks, under bridges, wherever – is taking your personal safety and putting it squarely in the hands of any person who wanders by where you are sleeping at 3:00am. No thanks. If against all sane advice you choose to do this, leave anything you don't want stolen in a locker, go in a group (with people you know well), and try and find someplace out of sight.

One option to consider before doing either of these things is sleeping at an airport if there is one within public transport range. Airports are always more isolated than train stations, and they don't get the late-night wanderers that train stations attract.

Some Accommodation Basics

Laundry

Get used to the idea of washing your socks and underwear in the sink and then hanging them to dry where you can contemplate them as you fall asleep. Laundromats, except in Britain, can be hard to find, and they are expensive everywhere. Yes, laundry is a pain; yes, it's inconvenient and time-consuming; and yes, it's necessary, especially so if you're trying to travel as light as possible. However, you may adjust your standards somewhat. Those who are used to washing something after one use usually go through a short process of reassessment in Europe, and after a week have made rules like: "If it's dirty, and I keep it in my backpack for more than 48 hours, it comes out clean." The usual tips:

❖ If you are staying in hostels, there may be washing machines available at stiff prices. Ask around if you can share a load with someone.

❖ The best way to dry something, especially in southern Europe, is to put it on you and head out the door. When it's 107 degrees in Seville, a wet T-shirt can be a godsend. Not advisable in muggy climates.

✧ A small (half-liter) bottle of dishwashing liquid with a secure cap is enough for one person (who is not overly fastidious) for about one month. Don't forget to tape the cap down, or else!

✧ Many pensions and family-owned hotels prohibit the washing and drying of laundry in rooms, although this rule is violated all over Europe. You shouldn't be too brazen, though, putting wet clothes on wood furniture, slopping water around, and so on. If you're clean and discreet, they probably won't mind. If they make a specific point of telling you not to do laundry, don't. At most hostels you could dry clothes on the flagpole and they'd hardly notice.

Showers

You will occasionally see some hostels or other places advertising "24-hour hot showers." They advertise them for a good reason: Some places only permit the use of showers, or provide hot water, at certain times. The reason for this is cost, since it is expensive to keep a tank of hot water heated during the day, when nobody is likely to use it. So, sensibly, the heat is turned on in the morning and evening, and off during the day.

Sometimes you are the person who turns on the heat. If you have a shower with an individual hot-water heater in your room, look for a switch, hit it, and then wait for about twenty minutes. Some places, but not many, may charge per shower. On the same subject, late risers in many hostels and small hotels can expect freezing showers that make glacial snowmelt feel warm and toasty. It usually pays to be the first one to the bathroom in the morning.

Eurotoilets

How can I put this? There are "facilities" in Europe that the average traveler is not familiar with, and may have to face at a time of desperate, diarrhea-induced panic. These are the bidet, and the two-footed "straight shot."

A bidet is that funny-looking oval porcelain thing with the faucet that shoots straight up. In the words of Crocodile Dundee, it is for "washing off your backside," and is also a primitive form of birth control. It is not for laundry, nor is it for washing dishes, nor is it normally used for an ice tub to cool off beers and grapes, although I have seen it used for all of those things. Unless you are extremely and justifiably angry at your hosts, defecating in bidets is not a good idea. The French love these things, for some reason.

A "straight shot" usually comes as an unpleasant surprise to most tourists. The door opens, to reveal not a lovely porcelain throne, but a very shallow basin about three feet square, with a couple of raised places to stand upon, and a small, evil-smelling hole leading to a seething pit too horrible to contemplate. Evidence of the aiming ability, kidney function, and recent diet of the last five or six users can be all too apparent. Toilet paper may be only an ancient memory.

These facilities (the norm for most of the world, by the way) are most common in France and southern Europe. They may make an appearance in public toilets anywhere, however, as they are cheap, easy to clean and maintain, and difficult to vandalize. If you don't like them, realize that the other option would probably be no facilities at all. Call it a cultural experience, and mind your aim. Using one of these while drunk and balance-impaired can have disastrous consequences.

One Final Thought . . .

No matter where you stay, write down the name and address of the place, and take it with you when you head out for the first few times. As ridiculous as it may sound, it is very easy to forget exactly where you are staying, since many hostels have similar names and may be packed into the same general area. If alcohol is involved, it is even easier. Yes, I have done this, and it's finally funny now . . . ten years later.

CHAPTER NINE

MONEY MATTERS

There are three perennial issues concerning money while traveling in Europe: How much do I need, in what form should I carry it, and how can I best exchange the myriad of different currencies used in Europe? These three subjects, and particularly the last two, can cause no end of headaches and extra expense. For example, if the first place you trade money is in a hotel and you get into the habit of doing so, it will cost you big, big bucks by the end of your trip. "How much should I take?" was dealt with in Chapter 3; now it's time to fight it out with the other two issues.

Changing Money

If you were to travel 450 miles from Milan to Amsterdam (roughly equal to San Francisco to Los Angeles), and stop in each country along the way, you would need no less than six currencies: Italian lire, Swiss francs, French francs, Luxembourg francs, Belgian francs, and Dutch guilders. Throughout Europe there are tens of thousands of people who work every day at nothing more than exchanging different kinds of money, and taking a percentage for doing so. What all this means to you is that changing money is going to be an issue, and can be a major hassle and a surprisingly large part of your budget if you're not careful. When changing money you will lose value in any one of four different ways:

1. **With a percentage of the total amount changed.**
2. **With a flat fee.**
3. **With a minimum fee.**
4. **With the exchange rate itself.**

Here's an example:

Bank A is offering a rate of 1.6 German marks per dollar, with a 3 mark minimum fee or a 1 percent commission.
Bank B is offering a rate of 1.65 German marks per dollar, with a 2 percent commission or a 1 mark minimum fee.
Which is the better deal for changing fifty dollars? *

I'll bet 95 percent of you just had your eyes glaze over. Seems like those miserable word problems you thought you left behind in high school doesn't it?

Who needs this crap on vacation? You arrive at a train station tired, hot, and sweaty, and you've got to deal with this nonsense, and when you do, you still have the feeling that you've been taken. So remember the following:

◆ When trying to compare two money-changing facilities, forget about the advertised rates. Ask the question: "If I give you this many dollars, how many francs, marks, pounds will you give me after all of your fees and commissions?" That's the bottom line.

---

* The answer is that Bank B is the winner. Bank A will charge its minimum fee of 3 marks, since the commission of 0.8 marks (1 percent of 50 x 1.6) is less than its minimum fee. Bank B will charge 1.65 marks (2 percent of 50 x 1.65) since 1.65 is greater than its minimum fee. So for $50, Bank B is better. Be careful, though. To change $500, Bank A is better, and will only charge 8 marks, while Bank B will charge 16.5 marks. For large amounts, Bank A wins by a mile.

❖ Money-changing facilities at airports and at borders almost always have very poor rates and/or high fees. If you have to use them, try and find one with low fees and only exchange enough money to get you through your first night, or to a bank.

❖ In general, for a small amount, like twenty dollars, look for low or no fees. For large amounts, look for a good exchange rate.

❖ Banks, larger the better, are almost always the best places to change money. They may not be in the train station with flashing rate boards, but they will have the lowest fees and the best rates. It is worth your while leaving the train station to find one, especially for changing large amounts. (Holland is a notable exception to this rule, where all medium to large-size train stations have change booths that charge the same as any bank.)

❖ Change bureaux are much more slippery and hard to pin down than banks. Beware of large minimum fees: a two-pound minimum will cost you more than 30 percent of your money if you only change ten dollars.

❖ Hotels and hostels almost always have the worst rates, but may not charge a fee at all, and can be good if you have only a small amount to change. Just don't use them too much.

❖ It is always better to change one hundred dollars than to change fifty on two separate occasions. If you are traveling in a group, change all your money together, and only pay the fee once.

❖ Larger denomination dollar bills and travelers' checks – one hundreds and occasionally fifties – sometimes get a slightly better rate than smaller amounts.

WARNING: Once you have crossed a border, coins almost always become unexchangeable scrap metal. If you are coming back to a country, save enough to make a few phone calls on your return. If you are not coming back, change all your coins in the country that issued them, or spend them before leaving. International ferries will accept coins from both countries they serve, but other than this coins can almost never be exchanged once a border is crossed. You might be able to exchange larger-denomination coins at major international airports, but it's not worth taking the chance. A pocketful of useless change can be an expensive lesson for the novice traveler, especially with British pound coins (worth about $1.60) and Danish 20 krone pieces (worth a whopping $4 each). These make lousy souvenirs.

How to Carry and Access Money

Travelers' Checks

In my opinion, travelers' checks are damn near obsolete, a holdover from the time before electronic banking. Back then it was impossible for banks to efficiently communicate information about the validity of a person's personal check across continents. Since nobody wanted to carry big wads of cash, travelers' check companies could sell their guaranteed checks as a kind of universal currency. Well, we don't use dial phones and typewriters very much anymore, and that's how I feel about travelers' checks. It is often far simpler and more convenient to walk up to an ATM and pull out a few hundred bucks in local currency than it is to find someone willing to cash a travelers' check for a fee. Travelers' checks also have the drawback that you pay a commission twice: once when you buy them, and then again when you cash them – though this may be avoidable (see below). In any case, ATMs are sprouting up everywhere, even in small towns.

The one good thing about travelers' checks is that they can be replaced if lost or stolen, although this is not as fast, simple, or easy as commonly believed. Generally, you will need the serial numbers of the checks that were lost/stolen, and the date and place of purchase. If you do get travelers' checks, keep at least one list with you (separate from the checks, of course) and keep another list at home in an obvious spot. Study the refund procedures for your specific company very thoroughly before leaving, as they can sometimes be complicated. You can't just pick up a phone, say "I lost my checks," and expect replacements to be delivered to you in an hour. No way.

I would use travelers' checks as backups: bring about two hundred dollars in checks and hang on to them for emergencies. If you do, here's a hot tip: Don't get your checks in dollars. Even outside Europe you can buy them in pounds, marks, etc, and by doing this you avoid any conversion fee you would pay to exchange dollar checks into that local currency overseas. If you are spending most of your trip in one country, this could save some real money (if you're not, on the other hand, it's probably not worth bothering). Just hope the check company doesn't try to stick you with its own conversion rate.

By the way, if you're going to get checks as a backup, get *American Express*. Others, such as *Thomas Cook*, are far less widely accepted than Amex, and Amex has plenty of offices overseas. When cashing checks of any kind, you will need your passport for identification. And finally, it's "check," not "cheque," or I'll hit you in the neque.

ATM Cards

One of the most beautiful short train journeys in the world is the Flåm railway in Norway, which winds off a main rail line down a canyon to the tiny town of Flåm, which sits at the head of one of the most majestic fjords in Norway. After rattling past waterfalls, massive granite cliffs, and little postcard farms the train let me off near the ferry landing in Flåm. Near the dock was a little glassed-in hut with a foot of grass growing off its roof. Inside the hut was an ATM machine. Out of curiosity I walked in, stuck in my card, and walked out one minute later with a couple of hundred Norwegian crowns which would later be debited from my checking account back in Florida, at an exchange rate better than any I had seen in Norway.

Needless to say, ATMs can be pretty darn convenient; in fact, they're my primary means of obtaining money while in Europe. Some tips on ATMs:

❖ Check that your current card, or a new one you obtain for your trip, is connected to systems worldwide. Obviously this is essential. Connecting your card to the Cirrus or Plus system, or both, is a good start.

❖ Try to get a card from your bank that does not have a transaction fee. Almost all credit cards that debit checking or savings accounts will charge a fee or percentage.

❖ The obvious weakness of ATM cards is that you are extremely dependent on that little piece of plastic. For that reason, don't rely on them completely; always have at least one hundred, and probably two hundred, dollars in cash or travelers' checks on hand. If you have this much, and lose your card, you can survive until you get another one sent from home. That said, you could avoid such an emergency by bringing at least two cards that can access your account, and only carrying one at a time.

❖ Finally, visit ATMs during the day, and keep an eye out even then. Don't get fixated on the little buttons and forget to watch your back.

Credit and Charge Cards

Credit cards can be very, very handy for those with, uh, cash flow problems. I strongly recommend getting one before you go, even if it's only one of those Citibank cards that are handed out like party favors in student unions all over the country. The whole problem of credit cards as a way to get sucked into debt slavery is not the issue here; if you are in trouble in Europe, these can be a lifesaver. As a last-ditch disaster aid, a credit card is the next best thing to a hundred-dollar bill in your shoe. For an example of this, rent the movie *The Sure Thing*.

❖ If you lose a credit card, only look for an hour or two before calling the company and beginning the cancellation/reissue procedures. If you know one has been stolen, call immediately. Credit card companies are a lot better about taking your money than refunding it.

❖ Many credit cards can be used to withdraw money from ATM machines. Just request a PIN from your credit card company and you have another way to get hold of cash in an emergency. Expect to get nailed with hefty fees when you withdraw this way, however.

❖ To avoid coming home to overdue bills, leave some stamped envelopes with credit card payments with someone reliable, who can mail them off during your trip.

❖ Note that an American Express card, with a passport as further identification, can be used to convert personal checks into local currency at some Amex offices in large cities. This can be quite useful for those willing to pay $75 a year for a card. Card holders can also use some Amex offices as mail pickup points.

❖ Some people pay for most of their trip with plastic and avoid cash as much as possible. If you do this, remember that the exchange rate may change between the day that you charge and the day you get your bill, and may cost, or save, you some money, depending on which way your home currency goes. Also, if you use a credit card authorization for a deposit, make sure that the authorization is taken off your account as soon as possible, preferably while you watch. If you don't, it will stay charged against your account and reduce your available credit until taken off.

Cash

Money talks, in no uncertain terms, in the local language, everywhere in the world. Always keep at least some of this wonderful stuff on hand. Generations of travelers have been frightened into thinking that carrying cash while traveling is something evil by years of American Express commercials. Carry some cash beyond your daily needs, but don't carry too much. How much is too much?

I guess the answer to that is another question: how much can you afford to lose? Changing anything much below a hundred dollars at a time, though, will force you to the bank or ATM machine endlessly, and make you spend a great deal more in commissions than you need to. Also, a fifty-dollar bill, or the equivalent in local currency, stuck in a jacket lining or someplace else where you will not use it day-to-day can come in very handy, and not just in case of disaster. Public holidays, late arrivals and/or incompatible ATMs can all cause inconvenience. Cash-in-hand is the universal inconvenience remover.

Wiring Money

In case of disaster, you can have money wired to you, albeit in some major cities only, and for a whopping fee – usually around 10 percent of the sum being transferred. Upon calling Western Union, I was surprised to find that they have no service at all to Norway, and none to Gothenburg, Sweden's second largest city. Expect similar coverage in the rest of Europe. I guess they think that people only lose money in national capitals. On the plus side, the money can be there in minutes, during local business hours. For details of Western Union offices in Europe, their phone number in the US and Canada is © 1-800-325-6000. If Western Union can't help, you could try an American Express Moneygram. Their coverage of Europe is better than Western Union, but not by much. For details call © 1-800-926-9400.

The State Department Citizens Center for Emergency Services may also be able to help Americans get money while abroad or help out in an emergency. Be advised, however, that this office provided me with the worst phone service of any organization I contacted in writing this book. The most incompetent of the tourist offices I spoke with was light years ahead of the State Department of the United States of America in terms of professionalism and service. How sad. Their number, for what it's worth, is ©202-647-5225. Other nationalities should contact their embassies and hope for the best.

CHAPTER TEN

IN SICKNESS AND IN HEALTH

Why might you be more likely to get sick while traveling in Europe, you ask? Well, let's see. You're on the move constantly, you're under a fair amount of stress, eating unfamiliar foods at irregular intervals, probably drinking more alcohol than usual, inhaling mass quantities of secondhand smoke, sleeping less, and when you do sleep it's usually in close proximity to large numbers of other people. Gee, I wonder why you might get some sort of bug after two months of that.

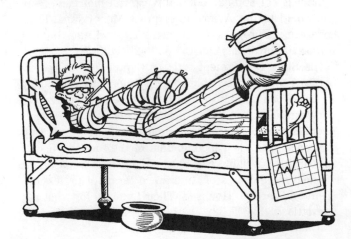

Despite that rather grim, but realistic, review of the situation, traveling for a summer is not equivalent to a death sentence by typhoid. However, recognize that your system will be stressed by a number of things, and plan accordingly. Stay well, rather than get well, is the best policy. Some thoughts on staying well:

❖ Heat, and staying hydrated, is definitely a concern, particularly in Greece, Portugal, Spain, and Italy. Most of the tourists wandering around Rome or Madrid in July and August seem to be carrying 1.5 liter bottles of water, which is a great idea. When it's hot, one of these bottles per day is an absolute minimum, while two is much better, and three is optimum. When you are moving around, and it's hot, it is difficult to drink too much water. Heat exhaustion and/or dehydration are serious problems, and thirst is not a reliable indicator of either. If you're really burning up, or you have symptoms like headaches, cramps, nausea, or vomiting, don't ignore them. Get to some place air-conditioned, get at least a liter of water and a pinch of salt into you, and start thinking about an emergency-room trip if you don't feel a lot better very soon. If you are older or especially heat-sensitive, this section goes double for you. When it's 103 degrees in Rome, take a taxi rather than walk two miles to the cathedral. Finally, there is a good reason for the tradition of siesta in southern Europe. During the blazing hours of the afternoon, a cool room, a shady tree near a pond or fountain, or in the fountain itself, are all good places to be.

❖ Tap water in most European countries tastes like skunk urine. It may be safe, and it *is* safe everywhere in Western Europe except possibly southern Italy, but it still tastes terrible. London water is particularly vile. Don't trust water in Greece, Turkey, Morocco, Eastern Europe, and Russia. Bottled water is available cheaply everywhere, although it will often be carbonated. To tell the difference, if you can't read the label, squeeze the bottle. Plastic bottles of carbonated water will feel harder than noncarbonated.

❖ Bring along some vitamin and mineral supplements, and (unlike me) take them regularly. Those in hard tablet form (not soft gel tabs) should be all right without refrigeration; call the number on the bottle to be sure. Also, bring along a supply of any drugs you need, and the prescriptions as well, to satisfy inquiring border guards. Check with your pharmacist on any prescription drug refrigeration requirements.

❖ The best way to prevent colds and most upper respiratory infections, believe it or not, is to wash your hands often, especially when you are living and eating among large groups of people. This prevents transfer of germs from hands to mouth.

❖ On one recent trip to Europe I went for an eighteen-mile stroll up and down hills on the third day of my trip. Needless to say, I got a set of blisters that made strong men sick when they saw them. I got them because I was stupid and lazy and didn't prepare for my trip by getting away from my computer and out into the world. Learn from my mistakes. You will be walking a lot on any trip to Europe, even if you're not going hiking: There are literally miles of corridors in the Louvre, for example. Take the time to get out and walk a bit before you go, preferably in the shoes and with the pack you are going to take with you, or you may be hobbling for your entire trip. I saw the Uffizi Gallery in Florence with a hole in the front of my right foot exactly the size, shape, and depth of two stacked quarters. It was not fun.

❖ A blister is a natural sterile dressing for the injured area. If you do get a blister, hard as it may be, leave it alone, and it will eventually take care of itself. Not always possible, I know, but still advisable.

❖ Sunburn, like blisters, can make your trip utterly miserable if you overdo it at the beginning. Some of the English and Irish tourists you'll see in Spain and Greece look like they've been sprayed Day-Glo pink. An extra hour spent in the sun can result in days of suffering. Sunscreen costs the earth in Europe, so bring a good-sized bottle of factor fifteen or better, and use it, particularly for the first few days.

- ❖ The Transylvanian Trots, the Hershey Squirts, Delhi Belly, the Orient Express, the Evacuation of Paris: They all mean diarrhea. Stay close to a bathroom, drink plenty of clean, bottled, or boiled water with a little salt, and/or flat soda (not coffee), and be careful not to get dehydrated. When in doubt as to the severity of an attack, there is no doubt about what to do: Swallow your pride and see a doctor. Greasy food, particularly that processed mystery meat cooked on vertical spits, is a prime suspect in this problem, as are salads, and drinks with ice if the local water is suspect. Plain, preferably live yogurt can be very soothing to the system if this occurs. If you are going out in the wilderness, especially in Greece, Turkey, Morocco, or Russia, some packets of rehydration salts would be a smart thing to carry, just in case.

- ❖ If you are getting sick, admit it to yourself and take a break. Don't catch that twelve-hour night train to Budapest. By taking a break, I mean spend a bit more money, get a single or double room, down a liter or so of orange juice and a couple of packages of yogurt, get twelve hours' sleep, and then take it easy the next day. Your body will thank you. Don't feel as if you have to keep going to get the most out of your trip. Visiting a museum while sick as a dog is not going to be a very worthwhile experience. Relax for a day or so, then continue the death march through the museums of Europe.

- ❖ If you are really sick or injured, your embassy, which should be listed in your guidebook, will be able to recommend an English-speaking doctor. Also, remember that the United States is the home of horrendously expensive health care. In Europe it's cheap by comparison, and may be free, even to travelers, in some countries.

- ❖ An insurance policy bought specifically for your trip is usually expensive in relation to the coverage provided, and may or may not be worth it to you. Travelers who are a bit older may wish to consider it more thoroughly. The policies that pay for you to be flown home are in my mind a dubious value. As long as you are in Western Europe, you will get fine medical care should disaster strike. Americans returning to the States may boost their hospital bill by a factor of ten. Before you buy a new policy, check to see if your old policy, if any, has something about evacuation already in it, or if an add-on can be bought for something less than a new policy. The prices on all these policies vary widely, and the coverage is often no better than what the buyers of ISIC cards receive. If you are eligible for any of the cards mentioned previously, buy one first and then see how much more coverage a separate policy will get you. Wade through the pages of fine print to see what you are really buying. For those with something that makes an injury more likely, such as a bad back or a knee that's been operated on, and for those interested in mountain climbing, kayaking, or other more dangerous sports, a policy to get you home may be a good idea.

❖ No vaccinations are compulsory for traveling in Europe that aren't compulsory in the States or Canada, though you might want to consider tick encephalitis (see below) or others if traveling in Turkey, Morocco, or the former Soviet Union.

❖ Not surprisingly, AIDS is as prevalent in Europe as elsewhere in the developed world. Make sure you're as cautious as you would be at home.

WARNING: For those going into the woods, especially in Germany and Central Europe, be aware of a disease called tick encephalitis (encephalitis is a swelling of the brain). Since it is spread by ticks, take precautions against being bitten, such as long pants, bug repellent, something to cover your head, and so on. Before setting out into the woods, get local advice from a knowledgeable source about the danger in a particular area. There is a vaccine for this disease available in Europe, but not elsewhere. It's probably worth getting if you're planning a camping trip to a high-risk area.

CHAPTER ELEVEN

COMMUNICATIONS

T he days of operators, transatlantic cables, telegrams, and all of the old images of communicating with Europe are gone with the wind. In today's information-driven world, Europe is only an electronic microsecond away. The mail can take a while to get through, but, except in some parts of Eastern Europe, it is almost always possible to call home quickly and easily. It's a small world, and getting smaller.

Calling Internationally before You Leave

Recently I spoke with a friend who was planning to leave for Europe two weeks later. When I mentioned that she should make a hostel reservation (she was going to start in Paris), she said she was putting it off until she figured out how to call. She had a point: I had never made an international phone call before my first trip to Europe, and I suspect some of you may not have either. So, to make that reservation before you head out, or to call abroad for any other reason, here's an example of dialing abroad to a hostel in Paris from the United States:

011-33-1-48-42-04-05

"011" is the international access code for dialing out of the United States to any country. Dialing this prefix puts you on the international lines. Other countries use different prefixes, and these are listed on the inside back cover.

"33" is the country code for France. Each country in the world has a code, and the pertinent European ones are also listed on the inside back cover. No matter what country you're calling from, the country codes remain the same – for example, the code for France is always "33."

"1" is the French area code for Paris. These codes may begin with a "0" if dialed from within the country, but this "0" should always be dropped if dialing internationally. For example, Central London's area code if calling from Oxford is "0171"; if calling from Kansas City, Kenya, or Singapore it's "171." Area codes should be listed with local numbers, or will be in the city information sections of your guidebook. The remainder is the local Paris phone number of the hostel.

Even now it still amazes me that I can pick up a phone and be speaking to someone in Paris or Rome in a matter of five seconds. Don't hesitate to call ahead for that first place to stay. If you don't call, you'll worry about where you're going to sleep all the way across the Atlantic.

Calling Internationally within Europe

Calling between countries in Europe is about as easy as calling between states in America or Australia, which makes sense since the distance is usually shorter. The procedure is exactly like the above. Each country has its own international access code (listed on the inside back cover); after this you dial the country code of the country you are calling, the area code (dropping the "0" if it is the first digit in the area code) and then the number.

To call that same hostel from London:

00-33-1-48-42-04-05

The *only* difference in calling from England is that the British international access code is "00" instead of "011."

Calling Home from Europe

In most of Western Europe you will be able to phone directly home in seconds. In Eastern Europe, some phone systems are more modern than others, and you may need to use an operator, or a direct phone service if you can't say "Please reverse the charges" in Polish. Your guidebook should give the details, as most of the less modern countries are catching up in a hurry. In any country where there is a real problem direct dialing, go to a hotel and ask for help. It may be more expensive, up to twice as much as a regular call, but you will almost surely be able to get through.

To call home cheaply, pay for a call or call collect only long enough to spit out your phone number for a call back. Call at a cheap time for the folks at home to call you. To call home, you will need the international access code for that country, the country code ("1" for the United States), and the area code and number, without another "1." To call information in Oakland, California, from Warsaw, you would dial:

00-1-510-555-1212

Direct Telephone Services

For those with *AT&T*, *Sprint*, and *MCI* credit cards, all of these companies offer direct dial services that can be used to phone home to the States or Canada. Those without cards can use these services to call collect. Be warned, though, that the *first one minute of these services will cost you a bundle* – as in five dollars for the first minute, and then about a dollar a minute after that. It is much cheaper to use coins or a card to call home, and then have them call back. If you just want to leave an answering machine message of "I'm alive and well," a phonecard or coins will save you big money over these services. For instance, I once made a forty second call from Assisi, Italy, to San Francisco, California, on a Sunday afternoon. It cost 1400 Lire – about one dollar. The same call using *AT&T* would have cost $4.38.

All these companies use the enormous fees they charge you to take out ads proclaiming how cheap they are compared with the other guys. Should you need an access number, remember that they are advertised in the *International Herald Tribune* almost every day. These companies also give out little wallet-sized cards with their access codes in various countries.

Time Zones

When making all of these intercontinental connections, remember your time zones: the Atlantic is five hours wide, from the East Coast of North America to Great Britain, Iceland, Ireland and Portugal. To everywhere else in Europe, add one more hour, except for Finland, Greece, Romania, and Bulgaria, where you add two more; for Russia you should add three hours. Australians should think of the bulk of Europe as being nine hours behind Sydney, adding on an extra hour for Britain, etc, and losing one for Greece and the rest. For all travelers, especially those from Down Under who deal with the confusing International Date Line, a dual time watch will make the issue much simpler – leave one on home time, set one to local, and you're good to go. Finally, remember to add or subtract an hour to that watch crossing the English Channel; it's easy to forget, given the distance you're traveling. As always, a picture says it better than a paragraph, so have a look at the map on pages 154-155.

European Pay Phones

European coin phones are usually a bit more sophisticated than their North American counterparts. For example, they allow more than one call per coin, which allows you to make a series of calls using one large coin, rather than having to scrounge for a bunch of little ones. If you have finished a call and want to make another, and still have credit showing in the read-out, press the button marked FC (Follow-on Call), or follow the multilingual instructions found on payphones in most European countries. If there is no such button, or instructions, just flick the lever down and release quickly. You should get a dial tone and keep your credit. Many pay phones will return unused coins, but they will not give change.

Once again, the cheapest way to call home is to use a coin or card phone, ring the person you want to talk to, and have them call you back. This is *much* cheaper and simpler than calling collect.

Phone Cards

Phone cards are very useful devices and are used all over Europe. They're little, prepaid phone credit cards that you pop into a slot in the phone rather than fumbling with coins. One of the best things you can do upon arrival in a country is to buy a phonecard, and use that to make your calls during your stay. Coin phones (instead of card phones) can be irritatingly hard to find in some major cities, and may swallow coins mercilessly (see my story about "The Tent" at the end of Chapter 4). Phone cards are usually sold through tobacco stands and news kiosks. Some can be quite beautiful and artistic, and when they expire they make neat souvenirs. Like postage stamps, some of the truly beautiful and rare older cards are now collectors' items and may be worth more than you paid for your trip.

Tokens

Some less modern pay phones in less modern countries, especially in Eastern Europe, may still require tokens.

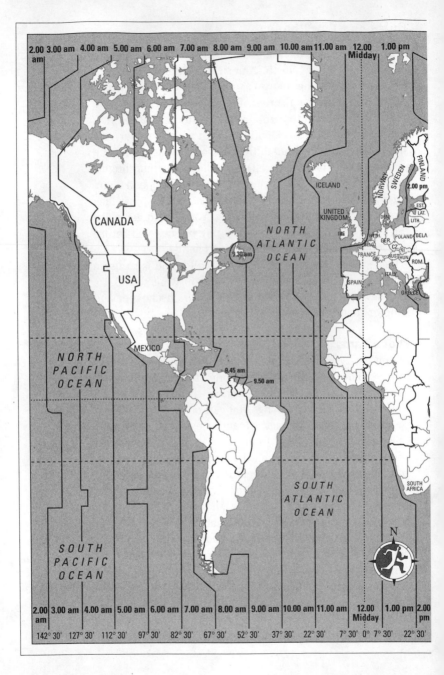

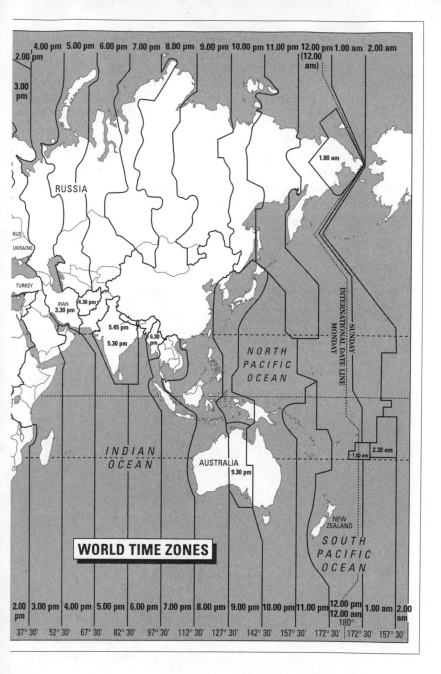

The tokens can be bought at the same kiosks and tobacco shops as phone cards. If the phone you are using looks ancient and refuses to accept coins, you may need a token or two.

Faxes

Fax machines are a very popular means of communication in Europe, perhaps due to the high cost of normal phone service, and they are available at many stores, hostels, and businesses. They can be quite useful for making reservations, getting information from embassies, touching base with home, and avoiding confusing phone systems (since someone will likely help you with the fax machine, they'll help you with dialing too).

Mail: Poste Restante and Amex

One of the great pleasures of traveling in Europe is sending rude postcards back to the poor, pathetic souls who are stuck at home while you travel. If you do this properly, your friends may wish to respond with some photos of your wrecked car – and they can, even if you are moving around. Poste Restante, or General Delivery, is offered all over Europe. Address as below:

Abraham LINCOLN
Poste Restante
Munich 1
Germany

The number "1" designates the central post office and may not be necessary in some countries. Use it anyway. Also, check your guidebook for information on mailing to specific countries: France, for example, requires a postal code on everything mailed into the country. Mail may arrive without it, but will probably be delayed. Leave clear instructions for the folks back home. Finally, it may have been better to have used the German "München" instead of "Munich." If you know the proper name of the town you're sending mail to, by all means use it. If not, don't worry about it – it probably won't matter a bit.

Officially, letters and packages will be held for two weeks in German Postes Restantes before being sent back, and will be held for at least a month in other countries. (In Italy they may be there until doomsday.) Unless letters are sent to a specific post office with a street address included, they will normally go to the central post office in the city, to the "Poste Restante" window or desk. When picking up your mail, bring your passport, expect to pay a nominal fee, and don't forget to ask the clerk to look under you first name, your last name, and "M" for Mr, Mrs, etc, if your bills or junk mail are being forwarded.

If you have an American Express card or travelers' checks, some American Express offices will hold letters for up to thirty days. They won't accept packages, though, because they claim to be afraid of bombs. Call American Express for a little booklet listing their overseas offices that accept client mail.

Mailing Things Home

Sending packages home is certainly possible, but can be very expensive if you want them to get there within a month. Sending things home by air is horrendously expensive. Sending things by boat can be remarkably inexpensive, but can take several months. When planning to do this, expect to spend some time in the post office, as customs formalities can take a while. Remember, the box or envelope you send will be beaten and battered on its journey. Use the strongest box you can find and tape it up very thoroughly. Wait until you get to the post office to do this, as they may need to look inside.

For those postcards and letters you send home, make sure you have enough postage – postcards are more expensive abroad, and do not necessarily use the cheapest possible stamp. Ask at the post office for the correct amount to get your card home, and remember to use the cute little blue "Par Avion" stickers. These stickers, and stamps, can be purchased at tobacco shops in most countries.

● ●

THE UNCLAIMED PACKAGE STOREROOM: WHERE TIME HAS NO MEANING

I went to a post office in Rome expecting a package to be waiting for me. It wasn't. The clerk helpfully pointed me outside and toward another door in the side of the building. When I entered, I thought I had mistakenly walked into the employees' lounge. Two men were playing chess, one was dozing in his chair, two others were reading quietly. After smiles of welcome and some Spanish/Italian/English communication, I realized that I was in the unclaimed package storeroom. I mentioned my search and was politely invited to sit down and relax. The warm air in the office was heavy and still, smelling of paper and ink . . . the chair was actually quite comfortable . . . the clock in the office was broken, but that really didn't matter much. Time seemed irrelevant in that room. I became mildly interested in the chess game. All was quiet, as if sound was somehow muffled. When I woke up, I was almost sorry to see one of my new friends standing there with my package in hand. Had he not found it, I might still be in that room. I signed an old ledger the size of a dictionary, waved good-bye, and stepped back into the real world. Outside, the traffic was flowing and the usual horde of mopeds was running like salmon. But inside the unclaimed package storeroom, in the Italian post office near the Spanish Steps, there was no hurry at all, and I don't think there ever will be.

● ●

Express Mail and Courier Services

For that emergency package I mentioned before, you might want to use some sort of express mail service. *UPS* and *Federal Express* can ship things to Europe, at varying rates of speed for varying rates of pay: $125 for a twenty-pound box of stuff, Munich to Oakland, in two business days, is a rough baseline figure. An eight-ounce letter will cost roughly thirty dollars for the same service.

The best services are *Federal Express* (℡1-800-247-4747) and *UPS* (℡1-800-742-5877).

Newspapers and Magazines

Both *USA Today* and the *International Herald Tribune* are widely available in continental Europe, for those who need a daily news fix. At roughly two dollars a copy, the cost can add up, though. Try the *Herald Tribune*, which has a certain snob appeal. It also has a decent crossword puzzle, whose difficulty varies at random from idiot-proof to impossible. Also, *The European*, an English-language newspaper that focuses on the affairs of Europe, is widely available, as are European editions of various British papers. While in Britain, definitely check out its wide selection of papers; to get both ends of the spectrum try the London *Times* and the Daily *Sport*.

A blizzard of magazines in English can be found all over Europe, with *Time* and *Newsweek* on sale pretty much everywhere. Also, try the foreign versions of well-known American magazines and note the differences. For example, British *Cosmopolitan* is so brainless and sex-obsessed that it makes the American version look like something written by Dickens.

"Listings" Magazines and Tourist Publications
Listings magazines, written in English, are designed to alert tourists (and residents for that matter) to what's happening during a given week or month in a particular city. *Time Out* in London is the granddaddy of these and

is about as complete a guide to a city as you're likely to find (it also publishes a version in Amsterdam, and an English supplement in Paris). Other cities usually have some sort of tourist publication, varying from full-sized magazines to small pamphlets, often titled "What's On . . . " (Munich, Copenhagen, etc). They can be useful for spotting events and for getting an up-to-date list of night spots, and are usually worth a look. Most of them are distributed to hotels and hostels or can be found at tourist information centers. In addition, most accommodations have the dreaded "tacky brochure rack," full of amazing attractions ("See the World's Largest Mayonnaise Factory! Free Samples for All"). Kidding aside, these displays are well worth a look to see if something strikes your fancy.

CHAPTER TWELVE

CRIME, SAFETY, AND SLEAZE

Europe is extremely safe on the whole – probably much safer than home if you come from a big American city. Nevertheless, petty crime against tourists does happen, and has happened to me. Crime is something you should be aware of; be prepared, but not paranoid. Rather than gloss over the problem for fear of frightening you, I'll give you all of the gory details – forewarned is forearmed. In all cases, an ounce of prevention is worth a kilogram of cure.

Notice how many of the problems below are prevented by using a money belt or neck wallet inside your clothes. This is your first line of defense, and it is very effective. To avoid having to snake-charm your way into your money belt every time you buy a drink on the street, carry a cheap wallet or coin purse with about ten dollars in it in a front pocket. This prevents you from having to flash the location of your cash in public places.

Theft on Trains

Robbery on trains happens fairly often, especially in Italy and Eastern Europe, and especially on night trains. Once, when getting off a night train to Naples one morning, I saw five people lined up at the police office to report stolen daypacks. Prevention is the key to this problem:

✧ Never sleep in a compartment alone if you can avoid it. This goes for both men and women.

✧ Always lock or chain your backpack to the luggage rack, even during the day, by as many straps as possible. That may be just enough to make a potential thief look for easier prey.

✧ Thieves prefer daypacks because that's where the small, easily sold valuables tend to be kept. When sleeping, put your passport, documents, money, and camera in bed with you, and fit your daypack inside your main bag.

✧ If you are in a group and you can't lock your door, consider having someone stay awake at night, especially in Eastern Europe.

✧ Top bunks are a bit more secure than bottom bunks.

✧ Don't be shy about locking your train compartment. If someone wants to come in and sit, fine – let them knock and wake you up first. If there's no lock on the door, use your own, or use wire or rope to tie the door shut. Once, on a night train in Poland, I thought about doing that and didn't bother. The next morning I woke up in Germany to find my daypack was gone. What the hell was I going to do about it? The train crew had changed at the border, and I was in a different country. By the way, I was a classic target: alone in a compartment on a night train, with the door unlocked. Don't repeat my mistake.

✧ Be very wary in and around train stations, especially if you have just arrived in town, are a bit confused, and are loaded down with stuff.

✧ Never, ever, allow someone you just met to "help" you put stuff in a locker at a train station. You will be putting it into a locker to which this person has a key or combination, and five minutes after your back is turned your stuff will be cleaned out.

✧ If you are in a group of two or more, and you leave someone at the train station with all the large packs while everyone else looks for accommodation, changes money, and so on, tie all of the bags together, or better yet, lock them all to something solid. The person watching them should keep a sharp eye on both the bags and their surroundings. I once saw a girl guarding four large packs. Had someone grabbed one and started running, she could either have left the other three or just watched him go. (Yet another reason to travel light.)

I'm sure you've heard the stories about gangs of professional thieves using "sleeping gas" to knock out and rob whole compartments (or even whole cars) full of passengers. Don't worry very much about stuff like that – it's neither very likely nor very preventable (although I guess opening the window couldn't hurt). Worry instead about the teenaged punk looking for a bag to snatch just before the train reaches a station, or the pickpocket looking for someone who has just arrived and is wandering around lost. Simply by taking the precautions just listed, as well as those to follow, you will be a much harder target.

Pickpockets

Here's my pickpocket story, which has a number of lessons in it. Getting on the metro in Madrid one day, I found the train door blocked by two men who just stood there rather than getting on the train. As I moved around them another man (who had just gotten on the train) walked out; as he went by he bumped into me rather obviously and kept walking without an apology. Such rudeness is almost unheard of in Spain, and not being a total nimrod, I felt for my wallet, which I was carrying in the front pocket of my shorts. It was gone. I immediately ran after the guy, got right behind him, and used my Spanish to call him a thief, a son of a whore, and other gross profanities. He kept walking without looking back. This convinced me beyond doubt that he was a thief, as any innocent Spanish man called such things would have fought me on the spot. After a few more seconds of being called a male prostitute, my new friend threw my wallet in one direction and took off in another. When I recovered it, every peseta was in place, and virtue had triumphed over the forces of evil.

All well and good, you may say. Except that I did everything wrong, and could very well have been seriously injured. The whole situation would never have occurred had I been using a money belt – the most obvious of security precautions. Those three guys wouldn't have even considered me as a target. Second, following the thief as closely and insulting him as thoroughly as I did was asking for him to pull a knife. A far better tactic would have been to follow at a good distance and shout for a policeman as loudly as possible. I got lucky. Learn from my mistakes.

◇ Every serious traveler uses a money belt or neck wallet. Again, highly recommended.
◇ If you must wear a fanny pack, wear it in front. Three seconds on a crowded bus, train, or street are all a thief needs to slash and empty your pack.
◇ Unless you really need all of those credit cards, leave them locked up wherever you're staying, or in a money belt – whichever feels safer.

Kids and Snatch Thieves

I have heard more firsthand stories of robbery by gangs of kids, often gypsies, than any other type of crime. The tactic is simple: Five or six small children run up to you, shouting and waving newspapers or pieces of cardboard. As they swarm around and distract you, your wallet/purse and the contents of your fanny/daypack are swiped, and off they run in three different directions. Elapsed time: six seconds. I've seen it happen, most commonly in Italy, less so in France.

If this happens to you, don't just stand there. Move away from the brats, yell at them to get away, and don't be shy about letting loose some slaps or shoves at any kid within range. Remember, these are not innocent tykes. They are professionally trained thieves, who will clean you out before you can blink. As with pickpockets, though, prevention is the best defense; a money belt inside your clothing is a million times safer than a purse or fanny pack.

Snatch thieves specialize in surprise tactics – grabbing cameras, bags, and packs from the non-alert and from those whom they have deliberately distracted. One woman I met had just gotten on a train when she felt hand cream or suntan lotion splatter on the back of her legs. When she put down her daypack and turned to wipe it off, the thief grabbed her pack and was gone in a flash. Variations on this include moped-riding purse-snatchers, camera thieves, etc.

❖ In any crowded area, such as on public transportation, carry your daypack in front of you.

❖ Should you be shoved, distracted, splattered, whatever, grab hold of whatever you have.

❖ Wear cameras and shoulder bags across your body rather than over a shoulder, and on the side away from the street.

❖ Don't carry a purse. If you must, and you really shouldn't, don't carry anything important in it. If someone grabs it and starts pulling, scream your lungs out. If the person continues to pull, *let go*. Don't get into a tug-of-war with someone who is probably angry, frightened, and excited. This is especially the case if the thief is on a moped, motorcycle, or in a car, in which case you should let go *immediately*. Don't risk a serious

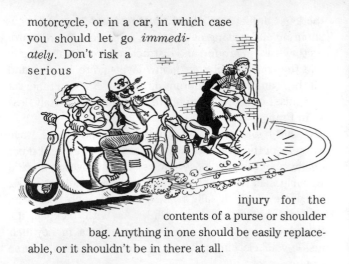

injury for the contents of a purse or shoulder bag. Anything in one should be easily replaceable, or it shouldn't be in there at all.

Theft from Cars

Rental cars are viewed by thieves the world over as mobile piggy banks. Tactics for crime prevention with cars are simple:

◇ Try not to rent or buy a car without a separate, lockable trunk. Be advised that this can be difficult. The smallest and cheapest rental cars are usually hatchbacks.

◇ Never park a car, especially a rental car, with anything of the slightest value visible inside. It is even worth pulling out the cover to the back of a hatchback to demonstrate its emptiness.

◇ At night, even though it's a royal pain in the neck, carry everything you can't afford to lose up to your room, lock the rest in the trunk, and leave the glove compartment open and empty.

◇ On the road, especially in a rental car, beware if someone motions you to pull over, especially if you are female, and especially if two or more males are in the other car. If your car is running well, pull over at the next gas station, if at all.

A TALE OF AUTOMOTIVE
WOE IN AMSTERDAM

A friend of mine and a person she met while in Europe recently drove into Amsterdam to go to the visitors' bureau. As they got out of their car, her friend said, "Hey, should we take our packs?" She said, "Naw, they weigh a ton, and we'll only be gone a few minutes." Twenty minutes later they returned to find the car cleaned out: Both packs, as well as everything else of value, were gone. The most tragic part was that I had loaned her my backpack for the trip! Poor Jennifer did a number of things right and a number of things wrong that day, and they make for good examples for any traveler.

Wrong . . .

1. Driving a rental car into the center of Amsterdam.
2. Ignoring the windshield sticker that warned (in English!) about leaving things in the car.
3. By not packing light, her backpack was too heavy to carry comfortably, which resulted in her leaving it in the car.

Right . . .

1. Immediately after discovering the theft, the two of them searched the surrounding neighborhood. Thieves will often clean out the money and small valuables, and dump the pack and/or its other contents. Searching is not, however, advisable at night, or in a particularly dangerous area.
2. She reported the theft to the police, who would then be able to contact her in case someone else found her pack. For this reason, she stayed in Amsterdam for a couple of days. She might also have been able to file a claim on her insurance policy, and would have needed the police report.
3. She took her daypack, which included her money, passport, camera and other small, valuable stuff, with her to the tourist office.
4. She didn't let the theft ruin her trip, and still managed to enjoy herself during her remaining time in Europe (maybe because she was traveling pretty darn light by this time).
5. She bought me a new pack!

Theft from Hostels

Theft from hostels happens occasionally, and is particularly galling because you know that a fellow budget traveler, who should understand your situation, is most likely the thief.

✦ If lockers are available, use them. Be warned, though, that those little locks that are so handy for locking up a backpack are inadequate for this task, and can be easily broken. Also, the key to someone else's little lock may very well open yours. I found this out when I opened what I thought was my locker and found a nice new camera that definitely wasn't mine. You can bet that thieves are aware of this fact.

✦ If lockers are not available, chain your backpack to your bed, a pipe, or something of the like. This will not stop a really determined thief, but it may make him pass up your backpack for another.

✦ *Never* leave a money belt, neck bag or wallet lying around, even for an instant. Do not let these out of your sight, especially in hostels. Leaving one of these unattended among a group of budget travelers is a guarantee that it will be stolen. Wear yours to the bathroom, take it into the shower stall, and when you sleep either keep it on or put it at the bottom of your sleep sack or sleeping bag.

Theft in Other Accommodations

When people stay in hostels, they are usually on their toes, if only because there are so many people about. If you are in a pension or hotel, don't relax your guard completely just because you can lock a door. Never leave valuables lying around your room. Remember, at least one other person has a key. A friend tells the story of entering "her" room at a very nice hotel to find a couple sleeping in "her" bed. It turned out that she was on the wrong floor, but her key worked just as well in that door as her own.

Violent Theft

This is much less common in Europe than in the United States, and may even be less prevalent than in Canada. One of the saddest experiences of my life was returning to the States from a long trip, getting on to the Boston tram system, and feeling a prickling sense of unease that I hadn't felt anywhere in Europe, Russia, or the Middle East. Street crime does happen, however, and all the normal precautions apply in Europe. Trust your instincts. If a situation such as walking down a street, walking past a group of men, etc, just doesn't feel right, turn around and walk the other way. Be particularly wary around train stations and red-light districts, and it's always smart to ask in the local tourist office if there are any local areas that are unsafe. ATMs, at home and abroad, are a place to visit during the day or with a friend if you must go at night. On the plus side, muggers armed with handguns, UZIs, and AK-47s are not a major problem in Europe: Los Angeles has more handgun murders in a month than London does in a year.

One final word: If confronted by a punk with a knife, let alone a gun, don't play Rambo. Give the worthless puke what he wants as quickly as possible, and don't end up in a hospital over a camera or a few dollars. Any police officer in any country will advise you to do the same.

After a Theft

As mentioned earlier, if something is stolen, even if it's your backpack, don't panic. Yes, it's a hassle, but you will be amazed at how much better things will feel after a few days. Whatever you do, don't give up and go home. In the long run, that will cost you far more than the loss of your bag. The first steps that my friend Jennifer took after her bag was stolen were exactly right: Look around the neighborhood, if it's safe to do so, report the theft to the police, and stay in town for a day or so to see if something turns up. Beyond that, there's not much you can do to get your stuff back. If it's not coming back, I can only advise you to let it go, and try not to let it ruin the rest of your vacation. Easy for me to say, I know.

Your difficulties will be greatly magnified if your documents and money or credit cards are taken with your backpack. In that case, you'll need to make a collect call home in order to get your credit cards canceled and to get some money shipped out, followed by a trip to the embassy for a temporary passport. See the sections on express mail and wiring money. The embassy can arrange to get money sent to you from someone else, but don't expect any cash from them unless you are really desperate. The next step is to call the airline so they can issue you with a new ticket. In this situation, a hundred-dollar bill or fifty-pound note (that you sewed into the lining of your shoe or jacket) would be a major help. I do it.

If the above situation sounds unpleasant, it is. Remember what I said earlier about having a copy of your passport, credit cards, travelers' checks, and airline tickets taped to the refrigerator at home? In a situation like the one just described, that piece of paper could be faxed to you in half an hour, and make your life much, much easier. Packing a box full of stuff that can be shipped out to you could have you back on the road, ready to travel, in three days. After prevention, it's the best theft insurance I can think of.

● ●

TRAIN PASS REFUNDS

This topic is very nebulous, and you should get as much information as possible on the procedures when you buy your pass. Unfortunately, the policy on refunds is in flux right now, so I can't give you that much hard information. In general, though, if you don't use the pass at all, or if it is stolen before it gets validated, you can return to the place you bought it, pay a 15 percent penalty, and (eventually) get a refund. That much should remain the same. What to do if your pass is stolen or lost during your trip is less simple. *Always* file a police report that specifically mentions your pass as being stolen, and get several copies of it.

Report your theft *immediately* to the agency that sold you the pass, and follow their instructions to the letter, which will probably include making a written report at the nearest Eurail Aid office. You should already have a photocopy of the train pass, either with you or at home. You'll need it.

Above all, don't give up and consider your pass a total loss. If you are persistent and do all that the companies require, you will almost surely get some kind of refund. You will probably not get cash, but will most likely be given enough rail travel power to complete your trip. Be prepared to give detailed explanations and proof of where and how much you traveled on the pass, especially if you lose a Flexipass. Good luck.

● ●

Harassment of Women

Harassment of women happens, and I'm sorry to say that the worst place for it in Europe is Italy, followed by Greece. Foreign women are often shocked at the reception they receive in Mediterranean countries. (Turkey, Morocco, and Middle Eastern countries are a whole different world, and beyond the scope of this book.) Female tourists, especially those who are wearing shorts or skimpy tops, are seen as fair targets for verbal or physical harassment that may not be dangerous, but can be unrelenting, and can spoil a trip to some of the most beautiful places in the world. Obviously, I haven't experienced this firsthand, so my thanks to all of the female travelers who shared their experiences, which are summarized here.

◆ Traveling (and walking) in groups is better than traveling alone – much better. Walking or traveling in the company of a man works wonders and will cut casual harassment by almost 100 percent.

◆ Shorts and revealing clothing, especially in smaller towns away from the tourist trail, are like red flags. I know wearing long sleeves or long pants in summer when it's 102 degrees is very unpleasant, but that's the way it is. A long, light peasant skirt is a good alternative to pants.

♦ Any verbal response by you to a comment, noise, pinch, etc, is seen as a success. Silence, disdain, and a lack of eye contact are the best response to fervent declarations of passion. Sunglasses to prevent eye contact can help. An exception to this rule is the dreaded public transportation groper. In that case, a loud protest is best in order to embarrass your assailant into stopping.

♦ Do not share tables with men who ask to join you, especially if the café or restaurant is half empty, most especially if you are alone.

♦ With two women, holding hands or linking arms may help.

♦ The fake wedding ring trick has been mentioned to me more than once as a way to discourage persistent types.

♦ Really unpleasant men, guys who get grossly physical, or those who seem dangerous, are a matter for the police. Don't hesitate to call them. Also, an appeal to the nearest group of local women, if you speak the language, or tourists of either sex, might help.

♦ Getting physical may provoke a physical response: Be very careful with this. Women just don't hit men in some countries.

Terrorism

The odds of your being involved in a terrorist incident are roughly equal to your chances of winning your state's lottery. Don't sweat this one. One of the best times in recent years to travel in Europe was during the Gulf War, when tens of thousands of nervous travelers stayed home or went home, rather than face a danger roughly equal to the possibility of death by lightning strike. Go, enjoy yourself, and don't worry about it.

If you really want advice, here it is. Don't accept packages to carry if flying somewhere, don't watch a stranger's luggage in a public place if asked, especially an airport or train station, and move away from and report unattended packages to the police. If you're really pumping sweat on this subject, maybe you can try sewing a Canadian flag on your backpack, like 99.8 percent of the Canadians in Europe seem to do. They seem to think it protects them from something; maybe it will do the same for you.

Losing Things

Now here is a subject that I am truly a world expert on; the kind of expert Albert Einstein was in the field of physics. The result of losing stuff can vary from the mildly irritating – say, a pen – to the trip halting (a wallet, passport, etc.). I know, because during my travels I have generously distributed sunglasses, pens, Swiss Army knives, airline tickets, books, a camera, and other things, all over the world, to the delight of the finders. Even now, some guy in Syria is blessing the stupid tourist who presented him with a camera worth more than the average Syrian makes in a month. The bitter fruits of my experiences:

◇ On any long train or plane trip, where you're sitting for several hours, things have a way of climbing out of pockets. Well before your destination, get up, get your things together, and check under, in, and around your seat for anything that might be lying around. Do this if you change seats within the train or plane as well. Account for tickets and passports well before landing. Don't wait until the last minute and then be forced to dash out – that's a great way to leave something behind.

◇ Try not to carry more than one bag at a time. Put bags of things you've bought into a daypack rather than carrying them separately.

◇ If you are leaving a place, and have this vague feeling that you may have forgotten something, or that you used to have something in your hands that isn't there any more, *listen to that feeling*. Stop for a minute, check to make sure you have everything you came in with, and everything you took out with you in the morning. Believe me, that funny feeling doesn't lie.

❖ If you've lost something and there's no way of getting it back, forget about it, don't get totally pissed off, and don't let it ruin your day. My friends who read this will howl with laughter, but just because I can't do that doesn't mean you shouldn't.

Sleazy Europe: Red-Light Districts and Drugs

There are certain activities, and certain "special economic zones" in some European countries which are illegal elsewhere – hence they are damn near irresistible to some travelers. I have to admit that I certainly made a beeline for the red-light district upon my first arrival in Amsterdam. Rather than ignore the presence of such activities and places, here are my opinions on and experiences of the seamy side of Europe.

Drugs

No, Virginia, the smoking of hashish is *not* legal in the city of Amsterdam. It is, however, widely tolerated. Because of this, thousands of people come to this city at least partly to engage in this activity. Perhaps my opinions are biased, but I don't think Amsterdam is currently made any nicer by the presence of de-criminalized hashish. What started as a free-spirited Sixties-type scene has gotten a bit rough around the edges. Results include large numbers of burnt-out types hanging around the city, increased crime, as well as some seedy hostels that cater to those who come solely to smoke. Also, the presence of such large amounts of hashish inevitably brings a certain amount of harder drugs in its wake. If you have the desire to see someone shooting heroin into their arm, walk out of the back door of Amsterdam's Centraal Station any time after dark and turn right. All those empty sugar packets were not left there by coffee drinkers.

Be that as it may, if you desperately want to smoke hash in Amsterdam, there is plenty available. It is sold in certain well-marked coffeehouses. You should realize that even in Amsterdam, possession of large (in the opinion of the police, mind you) amounts of hashish, drug dealing, and the possession of any amount of cocaine or other "hard" drug, is treated in the same way as in other countries – arrest and possible imprisonment. Also, resale of anything you buy may or may not put you in the drug dealer category, depending on how the police see it.

In other parts of Europe, except for certain parts of certain major cities, drugs are much less available than in North America. In most countries the standard rule of thumb applies: If you are arrested for drugs overseas, you are in for the most miserable and dehumanizing experience of your life. Consider going into a prison system where you don't speak the language, have no constitutional rights, would be a member of a tiny minority, and might be held for months without even seeing a judge. As far as getting help from the embassy in the event of arrest: Not bloody likely, mate. They're barely civil to noncriminals asking for assistance or information. Travelers arrested for drugs are seen as a waste of their time, and treated accordingly. They will check that you are not being abused (by local standards), and inform your family of the situation, but that's about it. Anyone who thinks that they will work tirelessly on your behalf because you are a compatriot in need is kidding himself.

Prostitution

Along with tolerated "soft" drugs, Amsterdam also has tolerated and semi-legalized (certainly controlled) prostitution, located in its infamous red-light district. Although there are large numbers of "professional" women here, and plenty of red lights, the district is a major tourist attraction, and it is hard to get any sense of wickedness when tour groups of camera-wielding senior citizens come walking through every hour or so. On a Friday or Saturday night the women sitting in the windows under the red neon lights are outnumbered ten or twenty to one by young men wandering the streets gawking. The whole place is more bizarre and surreal than anything else, but the district is such a part of Amsterdam that it is a virtual must-see. The crime rate here is above that of the rest of the city, but it is still relatively safe.

Hamburg's Reeperbahn District is a bit tougher and seedier than Amsterdam's red-light district, although it is also a major – and advertised – tourist attraction. Instead of quietly sitting in windows, battalions of multilingual women patrol the sidewalks. The district is also the home of many normal dance clubs and bars. There are other, smaller districts all over Europe, but these two are by far the most famous.

If you go out for the night in the Reeperbahn (and you shouldn't go alone), beware: The oldest scam in the world has reached its highest form here. To wit: You are in a bar, or nightclub, and a very sexy but slightly tough-looking woman joins you at your table. She is dressed tastefully, speaks five languages, and is friendly in a way that, well, pleasantly violates your personal space just a little. Her name is Heidi, and she is busty, and she is beautiful. You, being slightly under the influence, decide that this person is attracted to you and only you. When she suggests that you buy her a drink, you do. The bill arrives with it, and you find that you have just paid no less than two hundred dollars for a glass of lukewarm champagne. That's not a misprint: two hundred dollars. This woman's job is to hustle you to buy those drinks, and she gets a cut out of the price you pay. And you are going to pay every pfennig of that price, because outside the bar is a little tiny placard with drink prices listed, and there at the bottom in teeny-weeny black and white is the price of a glass of champagne. It's completely legal. The police will be on the side of the no-neck bouncer. Call it a cultural experience.

Private Clubs and Private Thugs

While we're on the subject of no-neck bouncers, many of the clubs and dance spots in Europe, particularly in France and Germany, are officially private, meaning that you can and will be denied entrance if you are not up to snuff. Most have entry ages of 18 rather than 21; most also charge in the $20–40 range for entry, have a smoke-filled atmosphere that closely resembles a tear gas attack, and have dress codes beyond the means of a Rockefeller. Entry standards are heavily weighted against

men. (Women should breeze through if properly dressed, while the beautiful may get in free.) For rejected and frustrated men, be aware that the bouncers who guard these establishments are often little more than thugs in suits, and that they are happy to demonstrate that fact to you. If you are refused admittance to one of these places, don't get belligerent – just move on to the next place. Don't give these knuckle-dragging throwbacks a reason to get physical.

Dealing with the Police

If, for whatever reason, you manage to attract the attention of the local law enforcement authority, innocent or not, do not cop an attitude, raise your voice, or act indignant. Police, like everyone else, respond to courtesy and don't like rude people. The difference with the police is that they can do something about rude people, and you probably won't like it when they do. A smile and a cooperative attitude will work wonders. It is particularly important to remember this when dealing with the Spanish Guardia Civil (the guys with the leather hats), and especially any member of the French police force. If you get indignant ("You can't treat me this way – I'm an American") you're asking for trouble. This is especially the case if alcohol is involved.

Also, realize that, in the relatively law-abiding societies of Europe, what is considered a nothing offense in the United States or Australia may attract police attention. Once, on my way to the train station in Copenhagen, two policemen in a car pulled over and gave me a stern lecture on the evils of jaywalking. Not likely in New York or King's Cross.

At the Border

Most of the time, crossing an international border within Europe is a non-event; your passport will be glanced at and you'll be on your way -- sometimes, between Holland and Belgium or Spain and Portugal, even that won't happen. Be aware, though – an offense that may be ignored in a large city will probably be taken seriously at a border crossing, especially anything having to do with drugs. If you forget about that little bag of Amsterdam hash until a friendly canine reminds you about it when crossing into Germany, you have just become a drug smuggler. Even drug paraphernalia, used or not, will raise eyebrows if spotted. Border guards, unlike big-city police, do not deal with or arrest criminals regularly – their main concerns are stamping passports and catching senior citizens with too many cigarettes. Nailing a genuine drug smuggler will most certainly make their day. The absolute best you can expect if drugs are discovered on you is a long delay, a blitzkrieg search through every inch of your things, and denial of entry to the country you're trying to visit. The worst you can get, especially in Spain, Greece, or, God forbid, Turkey, doesn't bear thinking about.

This all may seem obvious, but in London I once met an American girl who cheerfully described how she carried marijuana in her pocket through Heathrow Airport customs. By-the-by, had you been traveling with this person, or even struck up a friendship on the plane, guess who could have been detained had she been caught. This goes double for countries like Greece and Turkey. Yelling "But I just met the girl!!" probably won't convince the border guard who has just arrested your new friend for drugs, and is now pushing you into the back of a van bound for God knows where.

For just these reasons, be very suspicious if someone asks you to carry something for them, especially across a border (refuse immediately and get the hell away from that person), and be careful with the casual traveling partners you pick up. Horror stories of chance acquaintances loading a kilogram of hashish into the luggage of their new friend before crossing a border are not just stories. This applies more to the serious trekker than the summer traveler, but it can't hurt to be aware of the possibility.

Don't Be Put Off!

Please don't let this section frighten you into not going to Europe, or into being overly fearful when you do. The two principal "Amazing True Crime" experiences I just related are the only incidents I personally suffered in multiple trips all over the world totaling somewhere around 35 or 36 months of travel. These trips included a great deal of wandering alone late at night through Naples, Moscow, Cairo, Rome, and other big cities, and never once did I feel unsafe or threatened. Admittedly, I am male, tall, and fairly ugly, but the fact remains that millions of tourists travel in Europe every year without any problems whatsoever. Just be reasonably cautious, don't make obvious mistakes that present easy opportunities for theft or invite harassment, and you will be fine.

Even more so than this, 99 percent of you won't have to worry about any of the drug-related and sex industry problems. Those of you that do will have to decide whether the possible benefits are worth the risks involved. Before you head-butt that bouncer, steal that pub sign, or sally forth in search of your drug of choice, remember that you are a long way from home.

● ●

ONE FINAL BORDER NOTE: ENTERING BRITAIN

One other thing to know about borders, and this goes for everybody. British Immigration officials have a very bad and very deserved reputation for refusing entry to those who they feel are coming into Britain to work illegally. They can, and will, on a hunch, refuse entry to anyone. Do not, under any circumstances, bring anything with you that might seem work-related, such as resumés, names of references, want ads from British papers, anything of that sort. I have seen them go through a guy's diary page by page looking for entries about how he was coming to Britain to look for a job. Those who look like Deadheads or are carrying guitars can expect major scrutiny.

This is the drill. When entering Britain you are there for tourism. You have plenty of money and plenty of credit cards.

You are leaving in one week to another country. You have a reservation in a hostel in London (really make one, not just for the benefit of the border guards), and you wouldn't dream of sleeping in the parks. Leave it at that. A wad of cash is a good thing to have with you if asked to show means of travel. If you really don't have a whole lot of cash, then a reservation on a train or plane out of England, paid for or not, is a very handy thing to show the officials. Do not kid around with these guys, especially if they start the third degree.

Don't judge all of England by them either; I don't know why they're like this. So many destitute Aussies, Kiwis, and other Commonwealth citizens come to Britain with legitimate work visas that excluding the odd Yank or Canuck is like picking individual stones out of an avalanche. Be that as it may, expect a hard look, and be prepared with a clean appearance, a bright smile, and as much cash and as many credit cards as you can get your hands on. And after you make it through, look at your passport stamp. In case you didn't get the hint, there it is, in black and white: "Employment Prohibited."

● ●

CHAPTER THIRTEEN

WHAT TO SEE

T he following are my totally subjective opinions on what I've seen in Europe. I haven't been everywhere, or even come close, but I have seen quite a bit. As I write this, a very good friend of mine is heading to Europe for the first time. The lists below are the same ones I am going to give her. In every case, no matter where you go, I can give you one piece of advice that will be worth its weight in gold. As I've said before, GO EARLY. For example, at the Uffizi Gallery in Florence one morning, ninety minutes before opening there was one person in line. Sixty minutes prior about one hundred people were in line. Thirty minutes prior, five hundred people were waiting, and, as the doors opened, at least one thousand people were in a line stretching out of sight.

I would advise arriving at major museums about an hour before opening time during the summer. That way you will wait roughly one hour in the cool of the morning, see a relatively uncrowded museum, and be on your way as the crowds begin to get bad. Also, at the Louvre you can go late, during the relatively uncrowded evening hours on Mondays and Wednesdays.

GOING EARLY PAYS OFF BIG IN ROME

The first time I went to the Vatican Museum I followed my own advice and arrived an hour early, with a newspaper and my journal to kill the wait. As I stood in my one-man line, a tour group came up and was admitted to the museum. I followed them in, thinking that my guidebook was wrong about the museum hours. When I got to the ticket desk I found that tour groups were allowed in early so that they could be shepherded through the museum for an hour or so before they were taken to the Sistine Chapel. Standing there alone in front of the desk, as the guard read a newspaper and sipped an espresso, it suddenly occurred to me that I was the only visitor in the museum not on a tour, and therefore would have the Chapel to myself if I could buy a ticket early. A few smiles, some broken Spanish/Italian, and a few thousand lire later I was race-walking to the Chapel, having been admitted by the friendly guard.

I had the Sistine Chapel to myself for the better part of half an hour; no other tourists, no cameras, and believe it or not, for most of the time, no guards. Completely alone. Even if this was a unique experience, I noticed something else. After the first other tourists came in (about fifteen minutes after the museum opened) there was still about half an hour when fewer than twenty people were in the Chapel itself. It was almost nicer with them there, to see their reactions.

After seeing some of the museum's collection I looked back into the Chapel at about 4pm. The entire floor, every square foot, was packed with a mass of people. Flashbulbs were going off constantly, and the sound of a hundred conversations was echoing off the walls and ceiling. I didn't even go back in.

I guarantee you that the first few people I shared the Sistine Chapel with early that morning had a totally different experience than those who came only a few hours later. It pays to go early.

THE SEVEN "MUST-SEE" WORKS OF ART

1. The Mona Lisa (Paris, the Louvre, besieged by tourists)
2. The Venus de Milo (also at the Louvre, also besieged)
3. The Winged Victory of Samothrace (the Louvre, not quite so bad)

4. The Sistine Chapel (Vatican Museum, Rome)
5. Michelangelo's Pieta (St Peter's, Rome)
6. Michelangelo's David (the Accademia, Florence)
7. Botticelli's Birth of Venus (the Uffizi Gallery, Florence)

All these works are very familiar, almost to the point of being clichéd, especially the *Mona Lisa* (the *Winged Victory* is that stone angel with no head, and *Birth of Venus* is that naked blond girl on the seashell). Since they are so familiar, and their image has been seen so many times, they may disappoint at first. The presence of scores of frenzied, camera-flashing tourists (as is the case at the *Mona Lisa* from dawn till dusk) won't help. If you go to see any of these works, try to be at the head of the line when the museum opens, go directly to them and then move on to the other magnificent works of art to be found in these museums. Do not skip them, however. All these works are surpassingly beautiful, justly famous and well worth seeing.

SIX FAVORITE WORKS OF ART AND ARCHITECTURE

These are my personal favorites with a brief explanation of each. Totally subjective, by the way, and in no particular order.

1. Velazquez's *Las Meniñas* (Madrid, Museo del Prado). The greatest nonfresco painting I've ever seen, and one of the truly great paintings in all of art. The unquestioned masterpiece of a lifetime by one of the true geniuses of painting. The illusion of depth the artist is able to achieve with a layer of paint on a piece of canvas must be seen to be believed.

2. Goya's *Saturn Devouring a Son* (Madrid, Museo del Prado). The work of an artist teetering on the brink of insanity. If you see this painting, you won't have to be told that. There is a painting of the same subject by Rubens, also in the Prado. Compare the two, and you

will understand how close Goya was to the edge. He painted this depiction of savagery on the wall of his home, for his eyes only.

3. Rubens's *Little Fur* (Kunsthistorisches Museum, Vienna). A portrait of his wife that Rubens painted for himself, and the loving care and skill he put into it are marvelous to see. It hangs in a room with other works by Rubens, and it is so far superior to them that it makes the other paintings look ordinary. A strong contender for the greatest portrait ever painted – the work of a genius, at the peak of his skill.

4. Leonardo da Vinci's *Virgin of the Rocks* (National Gallery, London). One of two similar but not identical paintings – the other version hangs in the Louvre. The face of the angel, in particular, is extraordinarily beautiful.

5. The stained-glass windows of the Cathedral at Chartres. World famous for their astounding blue tones, this is only one aspect of a truly breathtaking cathedral located in a small town southwest of Paris. As my high school Spanish teacher said to me years ago, "If you are ever in France, please, be kind to yourself, and go to Chartres."

6. The Medici Chapel (Florence). Possibly the most over-whelming single room in the world, with four or five Michelangelo statues down the hall as a bonus. Built to house the tombs of the Medici rulers of Florence, and as an expression of their wealth and power. Look closely at the altar; what appears to be paint is actually mosaic inlay.

FIVE DISAPPOINTMENTS

1. Zermatt. The town, not the surroundings, which are beautiful. Zermatt is a town in the Alps very close to the Matterhorn, and has therefore been a tourist mecca for more than a century. For a mere $600 or $700, you can hire a guide to take you to the top of the Matterhorn. Plus the train to the town is private, and charges big bucks even with a Eurail pass. To top it all off, there is a thriving McDonald's in town.

2. Versailles. Didn't live up to expectations, but then the expectations are pretty high. Still worth going to see, though. The gardens are much better than the interiors. Worst food for the money I've ever eaten at the local snack bar, so bring lunch and spend most of your time outdoors. At this symbol of French majesty and grandeur, you are charged half a buck to use the bathroom.

3. The Louvre. Too big, too many tourists. Definitely go, but go very early or during the evening hours on Mondays and Wednesdays, and know what you're looking for before you go. The Louvre is best seen on two or three shorter trips, concentrating on a specific section each time.

4. Prague. Still a beautiful city with a wonderful atmosphere, but the cigarette ads, billboards, Pizza Huts, and other flotsam of Western society are disgusting. Prague will probably look like New York in five years, so go there now, and try and ignore the pollution that Marlboro and Camel spread all over the city.

5. The Olympic Museum in Lausanne. High tech and glitzy, but a bit superficial and very expensive. Skip this one.

SEVEN SPOTS THAT ARE TOURISTY, BUT STILL FUN

1. Neuschwanstein Castle, Bavaria. Make sure that after the tour you cross the bridge above the castle and climb up the hill for an incredible view. Lots of Germans visit here, too, so don't go on a weekend if you can avoid it. Long lines even during the week – bring a book and some water and food.

2. The Hofbräu House, Munich. Lots of tourists, but many of them, at least on weekends, are German. You will also see the occasional older man in full *lederhosen* getup. I am convinced that these guys are either hired to add atmosphere to the place, or else are mechanical dummies, like the Pirates of the Caribbean, and are actually drinking motor oil.

3. The British Crown Jewels. Absolutely massive lines, and you go past the jewels on a moving sidewalk/conveyor belt. Still, the diamonds are incredibly, unbelievably huge, and the Royal Punch Bowl is both beautiful and utterly tasteless at the same time.

4. The Buckingham Palace Tour. Another massive line, probably with the same people you met at the crown jewels. This tour may no longer be given, but if it is, you won't be disappointed. You don't get to look in the Queen's medicine cabinet or lingerie drawer, but the palace is pretty darn impressive.

5. The Leaning Tower of Pisa. Pisa is an hour from Florence, and best done as a day trip from there (about twenty trains a day). The Tower is actually the bell tower for a stunning cathedral, with a baptistry, on the same site (known as the Campo dei Miracoli, or "Field of Miracles"). The tower is really leaning over – if it fell over tomorrow, I wouldn't be surprised.

6. Pompeii. The ruins of a Roman city frozen in time by a volcanic eruption and untouched for centuries. Go early, and bring plenty of water; Pompeii is a huge site, and will take you much of the day to see properly.

7. Trevi Fountain, Rome. Almost everyone's heard of it ("Three Coins in the Fountain"), and I've met many who thought such a "touristy" place was not worth visiting. Don't make this mistake. The fountain is a marvel – a perfect marriage of art and architecture. Beautiful by day, spectacular at night, it should not be missed by anyone traveling in Rome.

SEVEN FESTIVALS WORTH BUILDING AN ITINERARY AROUND

All these are great – but for accommodation at any you'll need to book way in advance.

1. The Fiesta of San Fermin, also known as the Running of the Bulls, in Pamplona, Spain. A massive party, with an incredibly dangerous but exhilarating five minutes every

morning. Every July 6 this festival begins at noon with a rocket fired by the mayor of Pamplona over the heads of a delirious crowd in Pamplona's main square. The next day, and for the following six days, at precisely 8am, six bulls and eight steers are run about half a mile through the streets of the town to the bull ring. Anyone who so chooses can run with them, although females are very unwelcome. If you want to see this spectacular event, come a few days early and look very, very hard for a room. I slept with twelve strangers in a three-bedroom apartment and felt lucky to sleep indoors.

2. The Edinburgh Festival. The official Edinburgh Festival, which lasts three weeks at the end of August/beginning of September, is a serious cultural event. At the same time, though, the city hosts a military tattoo, jazz and film festivals, and the Festival Fringe, with thousands of alternative events – comedy, theater, music – and pubbing and clubbing till dawn.

3. Il Palio, in Siena, Italy. As wild a party as Pamplona, but somewhat less dangerous. On July 2 and August 16 the ancient neighborhoods of Siena hold a bareback horse race in the main square, a tradition that dates back centuries. Needless to say, there is massive revelry before, during, and after the race. As with Pamplona, get there way early, look hard for a place, and don't be surprised if prices have tripled for the week.

4. Oktoberfest, in Munich, Germany. Don't be misled – the Oktoberfest actually begins in mid-September. Everything else is pretty much as advertised: huge tents filled with massive crowds swilling beer and eating chickens and sausages. There are plenty of tourists from all over the world, but that doesn't take away much from the atmosphere of revelry.

5. Festival of Avignon, France. Mainly a theater festival, but with the stunning backdrop of the city as a stage, and plenty of off-Festival happenings, the atmosphere is unbeatable. Lasts three weeks from the second week of July.

6. Holy Week and Feria de Abril, Sevilla, Spain. Holy Week or Semana Santa, from Palm Sunday to Good Friday, is

celebrated here with a strange mixture of extreme Catholicism and revelry – featuring hooded penitents and vast floats carried bodily by the crowds, along with carousing in the bars. The Feria de Abril, in the second half of April, usually follows soon after: a weeklong party of food, drink, and flamenco.

7. Roskilde Festival, Denmark. Roskilde, a small town near Copenhagen, is the unlikely setting for Europe's biggest open-air rock event, held during the last weekend in June. Tens of thousands of tickets are sold in advance, but they claim never to turn anyone away.

TOP TEN MUSEUMS and GALLERIES

These are the big ones – the ones you can't miss if you're anywhere nearby.

1. National Gallery, London
2. Rijksmuseum, Amsterdam
3. Uffizi Gallery, Florence
4. Museo del Prado, Madrid
5. Louvre, Paris
6. Kunsthistorische Museum, Vienna
7. National Archeological Museum, Athens
8. Hermitage Museum, St Petersburg
9. British Museum, London
10. Vatican Museums, Rome

FIVE UNIVERSITY TOWNS

These are all places where the town is dominated by the university: Try to get there during the European term when the students are still around.

1. Heidelberg, Germany
2. Salamanca, Spain
3. Bologna, Italy
4. Oxford, England
5. Cambridge, England

SEVEN WORTHWHILE SPOTS YOU MIGHT OVERLOOK

1. El Escorial, a monastery and palace about an hour outside Madrid. The tombs of Spanish royalty and nobility alone are worth the trip out, and the building itself is quite impressive. It is filled with art treasures, of course.

2. The Cathedral at Köln (Cologne). This is a hot tip. If you are going to take a train through Köln and don't intend on stopping, catch an earlier train, and when you get to Köln jump off and go to the cathedral, which is a two-minute walk from the station. Give yourself at least an hour or two, as this is one of the most beautiful cathedrals in Europe. Then catch the next train to your destination.

3. London's Imperial War Museum. Tons of real equipment and some very moving displays. The films of the liberation of Belsen concentration camp are about as horrible as anything ever captured on film, and are definitely not for children. If the British seem a bit proud of their victory over the Germans in World War II, remember that the German occupation plan called for exporting the entire adult male population to the continent as slaves.

4. Herculaneum. This Roman town was buried in the same volcanic eruption as Pompeii. As such, it is a similar site, but much less touristy. Excavation is still going on.

5. The Alhambra, Granada, Spain. The fortress of the last of the Moorish rulers of southern Spain, and one of the most romantic of all European monuments. Granada is a bit hard to get to by train, but the Alhambra is worth the trip. By all means, visit the gardens of the Generalife while you're there.

6. Luxembourg. This small country refers to itself as "Europe in Miniature," with some justification. The countryside, with its river valleys and storybook castles, is beautiful, and there is a small wine-growing region near the capital (actually, the whole country is "near the capital"). If you really want to get to know a small part of Europe, a two-week trip here would be perfect.

7. Auschwitz/Birkenau. Not in Germany, as many believe, but rather in southern Poland, about an hour by bus from Cracow. Auschwitz, the original camp of that name, is tiny, and was used to house slave laborers. When most people think of "Auschwitz," they are actually thinking of Birkenau, an enormous complex located about two miles from the original Auschwitz camp. This is the real extermination camp – see it for yourself.

THE WORST OF EUROPE

1. Bullfights. I love Spain, and some of my fondest travel memories are from that country. However, bullfights are, in my opinion, the unfair, unsporting and cruel torture of a fine animal. If you disagree, go see one. If you agree, go see one anyway, so you can talk about how bad it is with authority. Feel free to walk out halfway through.

2. Secondhand smoke. We're talking billowing clouds of nicotine death, spewed forth from every man, woman, and child above the age of nine. Well, maybe it's not quite that bad, but it's bad enough. You'll see.

CHAPTER FOURTEEN

GOING HOME: SOME TIPS AND A REQUEST

Sadly, every trip must eventually come to an end. Truth be told, many people are glad to be heading home after two months (or more) on the go, sleeping in a different bed every few days. Returning home should be a piece of cake for the now-experienced traveler, so only a few words of advice are necessary:

❖ Don't forget to confirm your flight back home, just as when you left. Remember, you must call to confirm within 72 hours of departure.

❖ Get to the airport at least two hours before takeoff, and be prepared to wait. Security and other procedures at most European airports always seems to take longer than expected. An extra twenty minutes leeway can save you a bundle of stress.

❖ Those planning to buy statues or bronze cannons as souvenirs, and (seriously) those planning to live in Europe for a while, might not be able to bring everything back with them on the plane. If so, you can contact a shipping company that specializes in overseas moves. The cheapest are in London, and listed in *TNT*, but businesses of this type can be unreliable. Do some serious comparison shopping, and ask if you could talk with some previous customers.

✧ Restrictions vary from country to country on what you can bring home through customs, but everyone seems concerned with tobacco, booze, and perfume. You are generally allowed, tax-free, one liter of booze (must be 21), 100 cigars, 200 cigarettes, and about 250 ml of perfume. Anything more will be taxed. Each country also has a limit on other goods that can be imported without tax. This duty-free limit, in local currency, is $400 in the States, $300 in Canada, £136 in Britain, $400 in Australia, and $700 in New Zealand.

✧ When you get home, be sure to use all sorts of foreign terms to irritate your friends and let them know that, yes, you went to Europe and they did not. Complain about the coffee. Whine about the lack of art and culture.

✧ If you intend to learn how to speak a foreign language, do so right away. Resolving to learn a language is very common among people who have just returned from Europe, and the ratio of classes taken to resolutions made is about one to twenty. It's zero to something large with me. . . .

✧ Start planning your second trip to Europe.

Finally . . .

Every author hopes that his or her book will somehow benefit the reader. My aim was and is to provide information that makes your trip more enjoyable and successful. If I did that, please let me know. If I didn't, then definitely let me know, and tell me what was wrong and how to fix it. Whether or not I helped you, this book is not perfect, and can certainly be improved when we come to prepare a new edition in a year or two.

Accuracy is a major concern, and I would appreciate hearing of anything I may have missed. Also, if you had an experience that would help others if they heard about it, please write. This is especially the case if you have some expertise that I don't: motorcycle tourists, hard-core campers, travel agents who can talk about airline tickets from a seat on the other side of the counter . . . anybody who has information that could help the budget traveler.

The best people to assist the Europe traveler-to-be are those fresh from their first trip, because they remember the problems they just dealt with. As a fairly experienced traveler I now don't have to struggle as much, which means that I can't anticipate someone else's problems quite as well. So, please help me help the next generation. Send a postcard or letter to the address below. The best and most helpful letters will get the writer a copy of this book (or any one of the Rough Guide series); and everyone who writes has my sincere gratitude. Thank you in advance.

Louis CasaBianca
First-Time Europe Update
Rough Guides
375 Hudson Street
New York, NY 10014, USA,
or
1 Mercer Street
London WC2H 9QJ, England.

FIRST-TIME EUROPE

THE BASICS

Listed throughout the Basics section are businesses and governmental organizations that have the job of providing you, the traveler, with service. Some do a good job, many more do not. I have tried to note those that provide excellent customer service (often at increased cost to themselves). Those that do, believe that in the long run, treating customers well is good for business and is the right thing to do. Prove them correct. Let them know you appreciate it, and tell other travelers about the company. If you receive poor service, don't patronize that firm.

1 VISAS

Visas are pretty much extinct in Western Europe but are still alive and kicking in Eastern Europe. This could change by the time you are reading this, but don't count on it. Regardless, get your necessary visas early. Most visas, though not all, are issued while you wait at any embassy of the country you wish to enter. Be advised that some embassies only issue them at odd hours or on certain days, and some require you to leave your passport overnight or longer. Don't buy rail-tickets or make tightly scheduled plans without your visas in hand.

WESTERN EUROPE
France and Spain require visas for Australians. That's just about the only restriction for residents of the five countries addressed in this book. Also, there is a two-month limit on travel in Portugal for Americans and Canadians without visas.

EASTERN EUROPE
Americans and Brits are pretty much good to go, while others take it on the chin. Still, don't let the trouble and expense of the visa process deter you from visiting the many worthwhile countries in Eastern Europe. Sooner or

later they'll realize, like Slovenia already has, that the increased tourism revenue free entry would bring, would more than make up for the revenue lost.

The following chart shows the Eastern European countries that require entry visas from the travelers addressed in this book. Find your Eastern European destination in the down column and your country of origin in the across column; an "X" denotes a visa requirement.

	AUST	CAN	GB	NZ	US
Albania	x			x	
Bulgaria	x	x	x	x	
Croatia	x	x		x	x
Czech Republic	x	x		x	
Hungary	x			x	
Poland	x	x		x	
Romania	x	x	x	x	x
Slovakia	x	x		x	
Slovenia	x				

2 RAIL PASSES

If you plan on getting around a lot, especially to major cities, you've probably made the right decision in choosing a train pass. The next step, picking the right pass, may seem confusing, but with a little time you should be able to pick a pass that suits your trip. The details quoted here were accurate as we went to press, but the exact prices and types of passes available change all the time. To get the most up-to-date information, call one of the agents listed at the end of this section before making your final decision. Most student and discount travel agencies will also have the latest price lists.

Remember that train passes are not good on metros and urban trains, but may be good on some commuter lines. Many super-express services, such as the French TGV, require payment of a small supplement. When in doubt, ask before boarding the train. Children aged four to eleven get most passes at half price but, as always, call to confirm for your particular pass. Some definitions before we begin the selection process.

EURAIL PASSES

All five of the passes below are good throughout the seventeen Eurail countries: Austria, Belgium, Denmark, Finland, France, Germany, Greece, Holland, Hungary, Ireland, Italy, Luxembourg, Norway, Portugal, Spain (except private railways), Sweden and Switzerland (except private railways). *Note that Great Britain, Poland, the Czech Republic, and other Eastern European countries are not included.* Fortunately, train or bus travel is very cheap in all countries not included, except Britain.

Also included with the train travel provided by these passes are "free" or discounted ferries between Italy and Greece (see the section on flying within Europe in Chapter 1, though), France and Ireland, ferries inside of Denmark, from Denmark to Sweden, Sweden to Finland, and several more combinations of the above. Remember the warning about "free" offers, though; anything "free" will cost you a day or force you to validate your pass.

EURAIL COUNTRIES

Eurail Pass: All of the passes below are referred to generically as "Eurail passes," but officially the term "Eurail Pass" only refers to the most expensive type of pass available. This allows unlimited travel in first class (or second class, if you want to sit there) during their time period – as much as you want, anywhere you want in the Eurail system. Anyone of any age can buy one. They are available in time periods of fifteen days, twenty-one days, one month, two months and three months. Don't just ask to buy a "Eurail Pass" unless you are sure you want one of these.

Eurail Youthpass: Like the above, except only available to those who are under the age of 26 (the day you validate your pass must be before your 26th birthday). Good for unlimited travel anywhere in the Eurail system, in second class only, and available in time periods of fifteen days, one month and two months. Because they are only good in second class, they are much cheaper than Eurail passes.

Eurail Flexipass: These allow a certain number of days of train travel within a two-month period: ten or fifteen travel days are available. The pass contains a number of boxes, one per day of travel purchased. Before you get on the train, you fill in the day's date in a box. The pass expires when all days are used, or at the end of two months from the day of validation, even if travel days are left over. This version is good for first-class travel, and therefore expensive.

Eurail Youth Flexipass: Exactly the same as a Flexipass, except restricted to under-26, and second class only. Same time periods apply, and they're much cheaper.

Eurail Saver Pass: This pass gives savings to groups of two or more traveling in first class. Available in 15-day, 21-day and one-month durations, the Saver Pass can save $70 to $130 per person, depending on duration. It's good value for couples and groups, but the users must travel together, so be absolutely sure your plans won't change.

Validating your pass: Before using your pass, you must validate it. Before boarding your first train, go to a ticket window with your passport. The person in the window will enter the date, your passport number, and the last date of eligibility of the pass. You are then good to go for the lifespan of your pass.

● ●

BEAT THE PRICE INCREASES

The prices of Eurail and other train passes are increased every year on January 1st. You then usually have six months after purchasing your pass before you must validate it. (For example, if you buy it on December 17th, you have until June 17th to start using it.) What this means is that those who intend on starting their train travel before July 1 can save money by buying their tickets before the prices go up.

Before you do this, be very sure that you are willing to start using the pass before July 1. If you're not sure, it may not be worth the $40–100 you can save, but for those intending on traveling in early June or sooner, this one is a no-brainer. As always, there may be passes that are an exception to the six-month validation rule, so check with your vendor.

● ●

REGIONAL AND COUNTRY PASSES

Since the various Eurail passes are valid all over Europe, they are the most expensive passes available. You're paying for the right to use an enormous system of railroads, from Portugal to Hungary, and from Norway to Greece and Sicily. It's possible that you might not need all that travel power, and don't want to pay for it. If this is the case, you're in luck, because passes for smaller parts of Europe and for individual countries are also available.

Europasses: These are like a scaled-down version of the Eurail Flexipass, good for only part of the seventeen-country system. They offer a certain number of travel days in a two-month period, just like Flexipasses, but can only be used in a minimum of five and a maximum of twelve countries. The five 'base' countries are France, Germany, Italy, Spain, and Switzerland. For extra fees you can add 1. The Benelux countries, 2. Austria and Hungary, 3. Greece, 4. Portugal. By the

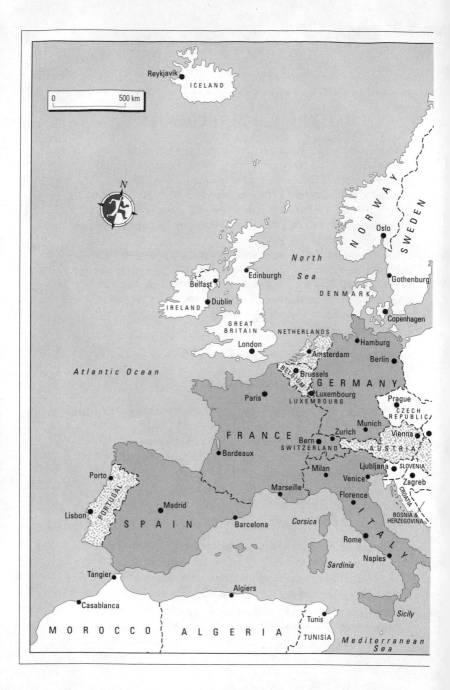

EUROPASS COUNTRIES

KEY:

EUROPASS MEMBERS

ASSOCIATE MEMBERS

FINLAND

Helsinki

St Petersburg

Stockholm

Tallinn

ESTONIA

Baltic Sea

Riga

LATVIA

Moscow

LITHUANIA

RUSSIA

KALININGRAD Vilnius

Minsk

POLAND BELARUS

Warsaw

Kiev

Krakow

UKRAINE

SLOVAKIA

Bratislava Chisinau

Budapest

HUNGARY MOLDOVA

ROMANIA

Bucharest

GEORGIA

Black Sea

T'bilisi Baku

Belgrade AZERBAIJAN

SERBIA BULGARIA ARMENIA

MONTENEGRO Sofia Yerevan

AZERB.

ALBANIA MACEDONIA Istanbul IRAN

Tirana Ankara

GREECE TURKEY

İzmir

Athens

SYRIA

Crete Baghdad

CYPRUS

Beirut IRAQ

LEBANON

time you do, however, the cost rivals that of a similar Eurail
Flexipass. Note also that if you are travelling from, say Italy
to Germany via Austria, and you have not added Austria to
your pass, you will have to pay the normal fare for your travel
through Austria. Europasses are good for reductions on
some ferry lines between countries in the Europass system;
if your pass includes France, you get a discount on the
Channel Tunnel services. Europasses also have youth discount options.

Country and other regional passes: There's a bewildering
variety of passes for rail travel within individual countries or
specific regions of Europe. Scanrail, Britrail, this rail, that rail:
The number, type, and price of train passes can change drastically from year to year, so the only way to decide is to get
all the details from a vendor and compare. Some of these
passes are good for unlimited travel, some work like
Flexipasses, and all reflect the idiosyncrasies of the rail systems of the individual countries involved. Check out
"Freedom Passes", which give individual coverage of most
European countries, for three, five or ten days. When considering a one-country pass within the Europass system,
compare it with a cheap version of a Europass, to see if perhaps you could get a lot more travel for a little more money.
Beware: Some vendors may only furnish information for the
passes they sell. Call more than one company to compare.

The following passes were available for the summer of
1997 as the book went to print, but the list is bound to
have changed by the time you read this:

Austria
Austria/Czech Republic/Hungary/Poland/Slovakia
Belgium
Belgium/Luxembourg/Netherlands
Bulgaria
Britain (many types)
Britain/Ireland
Czech Republic
Czech Republic/Germany/Poland/Slovakia

Finland	Italy	Scotland
France	Netherlands	Spain
Germany	Norway	Switzerland
Greece	Portugal	
Hungary	Scandinavia	

INTERRAIL

InterRail passes are similar to Eurail passes in their intent (to get budget travelers on the rails), but different in operation, coverage, and price. There are also a number of restrictions – you must have been a resident in a particular European country for at least six months, and the pass cannot be used in that country.

EUROPE'S INTERRAIL ZONES:

Zone A Ireland
Zone B Norway, Sweden, and Finland
Zone C Denmark, Germany, Switzerland, and Austria
Zone D Poland, Czech Republic, Slovakia, Hungary, Romania, Bulgaria, and Croatia
Zone E France, Belgium, The Netherlands, and Luxembourg
Zone F Spain, Portugal, and Morocco
Zone G Italy, Slovenia, Greece, and Turkey (includes ADN/HML ferr service between Brindisi, italy, and Patras, Greece).

Prices

Any I zone: £185 for fifteen days.
Any 2 zones: £220 for one month.
Any 3 zones: £245 for one month.
All zones: £275 for one month.

InterRail 26+

15-day pass: £215.
One-month pass: £275.

However, the prices are very competitive. The system divides the countries of Europe into a series of zones. You pay according to the number of zones you wish to travel in, ranging from £185 for a 15-day ticket that includes just one zone to £275 for a one-month pass that includes all zones. Like Eurail passes, there are options for under-26 and 26 and over. However, over-26 passes are only available for fifteen-day and one-month-periods (and cost £215 and £275 respectively), and don't include all 26 countries; indeed, frustratingly, they miss out key countries like France, Spain and Italy. On both kinds of pass, there are discounts ranging from 30 to 50 percent on ferry lines all over Europe.

CHOOSING A RAILPASS

When deciding which pass is right for you, the two questions you need to answer are (1) where do you want to go, and (2) how definite are your plans? Someone with definite plans has it easy. They can look at where they want to go and how much train travel they need to do, and use the price list to pick a pass that suits their needs. If you are sure of where you want to go, get the cheapest pass that takes you there. If you are going to be staying in one or two countries, you don't need a Eurail pass. If you know you are going to be staying in Italy and Germany, for example, a Europass will probably be fine for you, or perhaps even individual tickets. In general, though, I recommend regional and country passes only for those who are positive they will be staying in those regions or countries.

Most people headed for Europe aren't certain of their plans. They have some places they know they want to see, but they aren't sure in what order, and they may want to change their plans as they go. If that is the case, and you want the freedom to wander all over Europe if you choose, then skip the regional or country passes. The extra money you pay for the freedom to travel farther will be worth it. My advice in this situation is simple: for your first trip, especially if it's for a whole summer, get the most powerful pass you can afford, either a fifteen-day Eurail Flexipass or a two or three-month unlimited Eurail pass, and ride it into the ground.

Consider the following:

◇ I have seldom met travelers who have seen less than they intended. I know several people, myself included, who ended up traveling around a lot more than they expected. If this is your first trip, you will probably end up in places you never expected to go or never heard of until you got to Europe. I doubt you'll regret going for a more powerful pass.

◇ Regional passes don't save that much. An example of this is the Europass. In 1996 a fifteen-day Europass or youth pass for all five countries was only $88 cheaper than a fifteen-day Eurail Flexipass. That extra $88 spent could save you hundreds if you suddenly decided to go to Norway or Sweden, and you'd be much more likely to go because your trip would be paid for already.

◇ If you are intending to see a lot and cover a lot of ground, then the only decision you have to make is between a two-month Eurail pass and a fifteen-day Eurail Flexipass, or, if under 26, the youth versions of these passes. In 1996 the price difference was $210 if you were under 26, $336 for over 26. By their very nature, Flexi- and unlimited travel passes pull the traveler in opposite directions. Basically, unlimited passes encourage you to travel, because your trip is already paid for. Flexipasses discourage you from traveling because every time you travel you lose one of those precious days. In general, if you plan on traveling on a train for fewer than twelve days during the length of your trip, then a Flexipass is better than an unlimited one. (Allow three unplanned trips to be on the safe side, for a total of fifteen days.) If you intend on being on the rails more than fifteen times in two months, and that's not unreasonable, then go unlimited. It's a harder decision if you reckon on traveling between twelve and fifteen days, and you will have to do some more precise calculations of how much you want to travel.

❖ If you are spending less than six weeks in Europe, you would probably be better off with a Flexipass. Overall, fifteen-day and one-month Eurail- and Youthpasses are clear losers in comparison with Flexipasses. For example, in 1996 a fifteen-day Eurail Youthpass was only twenty dollars less than a ten-day-in-two-months youth Flexipass ($418 versus $438). And if you intend on spending more than ten out of fifteen days on a train, you'd be better off staying at home and living on a train for two weeks. For those over 26, a fifteen days in two months Flexipass is cheaper than the Eurail pass for one month. Even if you want to spend every other day for a month on a train, the Flexipass is cheaper. For shorter trips, where your plans will be more certain, Europasses and other regional passes may make sense. As always, think very hard about where you want to go, and whether there is any chance of traveling beyond those plans.

❖ While EU citizens and subjects are not eligible for Eurail passes (and with InterRail passes, who cares?), most national and regional rail passes are fair game for anyone not a citizen of the country selling the pass. As always, do some comparison shopping – find a pass that interests you, then make your inquries to travel agents before buying.

❖ If you qualify for an InterRail pass, bear in mind that the differences between the prices of the various zonal tickets is relatively small. Therefore, if you're not sure where you're going to be travelling, it's probably worth investing in an all-zone pass, since it gives much greater flexibility once you're on the road.

On a first trip, you are going to want to see a lot. As I said before, I know very few people who have gone to Europe and have traveled less than they expected. If you can afford it, and you have the time, get an unlimited two-month pass and hit the tracks. You won't be worried about saving days or traveling after midnight. If you are in Germany and decide you want to see the midnight sun, two days later you can be above the Arctic Circle. If you get cold while you are there, three days later you can be in sunny Spain. Having an unlimited pass in hand is a powerful incentive to travel to a spot on a whim. To look at a map of Europe and know that you can go absolutely anywhere you like is a great feeling. If you are in doubt, and especially for your first trip, I would go for an unlimited pass.

US RAIL CONTACTS

BritRail Travel, 1500 Broadway, New York, NY 10036 (℗ 1-800-677-8585). UK passes.

CIT Tours, 342 Madison Ave, Suite 207, New York, NY 10173 (℗ 1-800-CIT-TOUR or 212-697-2100, fax 212-697-1394). *Eurail, Euro*, German, Italian passes.

Council Travel, 205 E 42nd St, New York, NY 10017 (℗ 1-800-2COUNCIL). Student travel organization with many local offices, usually near colleges and universites.

DER Tours/GermanRail, 9501 W Devon Ave, Suite 400, Rosemont, IL 60018 (℗ 1-800-421-2929). *Eurail, Euro*, German, Austrian and many other passes.

Forsyth Travel Library, 1750 E 131st St, Kansas City, MO 64146 or PO Box 480800, Kansas City, MO 64148 (℗ 1-800-FOR-SYTH or 816-942-9050, fax 816-942-6969). Sells *Eurail, Euro*, and most other passes, as well as individual tickets, hostel memberships, and travel accessories. Also the best telephone service of the bunch.

Orbis Polish Travel Bureau, 342 Madison Ave, New York, NY 10173 (℗ 1-800-223-6037, fax 212-682-4715). Passes for Poland, also individual tickets and tours. Good phone service.

Rail Europe, 226 Westchester Ave, White Plains, NY 10604 (℗ 1-800-438-7245). Official *Eurail* pass agent in North America; sells the widest range of European regional and individual country passes. Horrible phone service, however.

ScanTours, 3439 Wade St, Los Angeles, CA 90066 (℗ 1-800-223-7226, fax 310-390-0493). *Eurail*, Scandinavian and other country passes.

UK RAIL CONTACTS

British Rail, European information line (℡0171/834 2345)

Eurostar, EPS House, Waterloo Station, London SE1 8SE
(reservations ℡0345/881881 25/1/96)

Eurotrain, 52 Grosvenor Gardens, London SW1W 0AG
℡0171/730 3402)

Wasteels, Victoria Station (by platform 2), London SW1V 1JY
(℡0171/834 7066)

3 NATIONAL TOURIST OFFICES

Below is a list of tourist offices currently operating in the United States, Canada, Britain, Australia, and New Zealand. In North America, many of these offices move around and change phone numbers quite often, so even the most current list may include a bad number or two; most of the US offices are in New York, so if you get an invalid number, a call to ℡ 212-555-1212 should get you that office's new number. Some countries also maintain offices in Los Angeles or Chicago. When calling these places, if you have a special interest such as biking or walking, mention it when asking for information. Ask for maps, too, especially for countries in Central and Eastern Europe, where up-to-date maps are often scarcer in the country than in their tourist offices abroad.

Many European countries simply don't want to spend the money to have tourist offices Down Under. There are a few offices in Australia, but almost none in New Zealand. In many cases, the offices are either linked to each country's major national airline or operate as part of an embassy. Even where no tourist office is listed, a call to the national airline (*Air France*, *KLM*, etc) or embassy may net you some information. These numbers may be found in any local phone book -- look hard for a toll-free number.

In a depressing trend, many tourist offices now use computerized answering machines to get information. If you do get hold of a person and he does a good job handling your needs, thank him for the personal touch.

AUSTRIA US PO Box 1142, Times Square, New York, NY 10108-1142 (℗ 212-944-6880, fax 212-730-4568); fax, phone, and mail only. **Canada** 2 Bloor St E, Suite 3330, Toronto, ON M4W 1A8 (℗ 416-967-3381, fax 416-967-4101). **UK** 30 St George St, London W1R 0AL (℗ 0171-629-0461). **Australia** 36 Carrington St, 1st Floor, Sydney NSW 2000 (℗02-299-3621).

BELGIUM US 780 3rd Ave, Suite 1501, New York, NY 10017-7076 (℗ 212-758-8130; fax 212-355-7675). Poor telephone service, but you can visit their office from 9:30-4:30. **UK** 29 Princes St, London W1R 7RG

BULGARIA US (Balkan Holidays) 41 E 42nd St, New York, NY 10017 (℗ 212-573-5530, fax 212-573-5538). Balkan Holidays is a tour operator, not a tourist office, but they do send out general information to prospective tourists. You can also stop by for info from 9:00-5:00.

CZECH REPUBLIC US (Cedok) 10 E 40th St, New York, NY 10016 (℗ 212-689-9720, fax 212-481-0597). **UK** 95 Great Portland St, London W1N (℗ 0171-436-8200). Cedok is a holdover from the old days of state tourism. They are not a tourist office, but rather a tour operator. They can provide information on and make reservations for hotels, airlines, tours, and packages, but they don't have general information on the country to give away.

DENMARK US PO Box 4649, Grand Central Station, New York, NY 10163-4649 (℗ 212-949-2333, fax 212-983-5260). **UK** 55 Sloane St, London SW1X 9SY (℗ 0171-259-5959). In the States, Denmark, Norway, Sweden, Finland, and Iceland share facilities under the name of the Scandinavian Tourist Board. They do not have walk-in facilities, but have great phone service. To request information on a specific country, call, fax, or write to the Danish, Icelandic, Finnish, etc, Tourist Board at the phone number or address listed above.

For general information, the office manager recommends you ask for the "Travel Directory" for the specific country or countries you are interested in visiting. See below for individual fax numbers and (under Finland) a free phone number. Open 9:00-5:00.

FINLAND US See Denmark for the address, or call ℂ 1-800-FIN-INFO. This number rings the same switchboard as the number in the Denmark entry above. And it's free! **UK** 30 Pall Mall, London SW1Y 5LP (ℂ 0171-839-4048).

FRANCE US 444 Madison Ave, 16th floor, New York, NY 10022 (ℂ 1-900-990-0040). France is infamous in the tourist information business for its 900 number. I hope it's not a trend in the industry. A friendly human being does answer that number, so it's not all bad. Other offices, at 676 N Michigan Ave, Chicago, IL 60611 (ℂ 312-751-7800, fax 312-337-6339) and 9454 Wilshire Blvd, Suite 715, Beverly Hills, CA 90212 (ℂ 310-271-6665, fax 310-276-2835), have computerized voice mail systems that refer you back to the 900 number for anything beyond sending out brochures. If you are in the vicinity of their non-New York offices, use one; the New York office is by far the busiest. **Canada** 1981 Av McGill College, Suite 490, Montreal, PQ H3A 2W9 (ℂ 514-288-4264). All offices open from 9:00-5:00. **UK** 178 Piccadilly, London W1V 0AL (ℂ 0171-629-9376). **Australia** 12 Castlereagh St, Sydney, NSW 2000 (ℂ 02-231-5244).

GERMANY US 122 E 42nd St, 52nd floor, New York, NY 10168 (ℂ 212-661-7200; fax 212-661-7174); 11766 Wilshire Blvd, Suite 750, Los Angeles, CA 90025 (ℂ 310-575-9799, fax 310-575-1565). **Canada** 175 Bloor St E, North Tower, Suite 604, Toronto, ON M4W 3R8 (ℂ 416-968-1570, fax 416-968-1986). **UK** Nightingale House, 65 Curzon St, London W1Y 8NE (ℂ 0171-495-0081). **Australia** Lufthansa House, 9th Floor, 143 Macuarie St, Sydney, NSW 2000 (ℂ 02-367-3890)

GREECE US 645 Fifth Ave, New York, NY 10022 (ℂ 212-421-5777). This office is on the fifth floor of the Olympic Tower, and has walk-in. They're very friendly on the phone. **Canada** 1300 Bay St, Toronto, ON M5R 3K8

(℗ 416-968-2220). **UK** 4 Conduit St, London W1R 0DJ
(℗ 0171-734-5997). **Australia** 51 Pitt St, Sydney, NSW 2000
(℗ 02-241-1663).

HUNGARY US 150 E 58th Street, New York, NY 10155
(℗ 212-355-0240). Walk-in available, and very polite and
helpful.

ICELAND See the entry for Denmark.

IRELAND 345 Park Ave, 17th floor, New York, NY 10154
(℗ 1-800-223-6470, fax 212-371-9052/9059). The overall
champion for friendliness and helpfulness. Walk-in? Of
course. **Canada** 160 Bloor St E, Suite 934, Toronto, ON
M4W 1B9 (℗ 416-929-2777). **UK** 150 New Bond St, London
W1Y 0AQ (℗ 0171-493-3201). **Australia** 36 Carrington St,
5th Floor, Sydney, NSW 2000 (℗02-299-6177).

ITALY US Italy has three regional offices, and they requested
that I give their service areas in detail, so that the New
York office doesn't end up sending stuff to someone in Los
Angeles. So: Alabama, Arkansas, Connecticut, Delaware,
DC, Florida, Georgia, Louisiana, Maine, Maryland,
Massachusetts, Mississippi, New Hampshire, New Jersey,
New York, North Carolina, Oklahoma, Pennsylvania, Rhode
Island, South Carolina, Tennessee, Texas, Vermont, Virginia,
West Virginia, and Puerto Rico and the Virgin Islands,
contact the New York office at 630 5th Ave, Suite 1565,
New York, NY 10111 (℗ 212-245-4822, fax 212-586-9249).
For Illinois, Indiana, Iowa, Kansas, Kentucky, Michigan,
Minnesota, Missouri, Nebraska, North Dakota, Ohio,
South Dakota, and Wisconsin, contact the Chicago office
at 401 N Michigan Ave, Suite 3030, Chicago, IL 60611
(℗ 312-644-9448, fax 312-644-3019). For Alaska, Arizona,
California, Colorado, Hawaii, Idaho, Montana, Nevada, New
Mexico, Oregon, Utah, Washington, and Wyoming, get
hold of the Los Angeles office at 12400 Wilshire Blvd,
Suite 550, Los Angeles, CA 90025 (℗ 310-820-0098,
fax 310-820-6357). **Canada**, 1 Pl Ville Marie, Suite 1914,
Montreal, PQ H3B 3M9 (℗ 514-866-7667, fax 514-392-
1429). **UK** 1 Princes St, London W1R 8AY (℗ 0171-408-
1254).

LUXEMBOURG US 17 Beekman Pl, New York, NY 10022 (✆ 212-935-8888, fax 212-935-5896). **UK** 122 Regent St, London W1R 5FE (✆ 0171-434-2800). Only one office for both the States and Canada, but great service and a helpful attitude; walk-in information is available. Open 9:00-5:00.

MOROCCO US 20 E 46th St, Suite 1201, New York, NY 10017 (✆ 212-557-2520, fax 212-949-8148). Walk-in information, and very pleasant over the phone. **Canada** 2001 Rue Université, Suite 1460, Montréal, PQ H3A 2A6 (✆ 514-842-8111). **UK** 205 Regent St, London W1R 7DE (✆ 0171-437-0073).

NETHERLANDS US 225 N Michigan Ave #326, Chicago, IL 60601 (✆ 312-819-0300, fax 312-819-1740). This office will be getting a new number, so you may need to call information. **Canada** 25 Adelaide St E, Suite 710, Toronto, ON M5C 1Y2 (✆ 416-363-1577).

NORWAY For **US**, see the entry for Denmark. **UK** 5-11 Lower Regent St, London SW1Y 4LR (✆ 0171-839-6255).

POLAND US 275 Madison Ave, Suite 1711, New York, NY 10016 (✆ 212-388-9412, fax 212-338-9283). **UK** 310-312 Regent St, London W1R 7DE (✆ 0171-580-8811).

PORTUGAL US 590 Fifth Ave, New York, NY 10036-4704 (✆ 212-354-4403, fax 212-764-6137). **Canada** 60 Bloor St West, Suite 1005, Toronto, ON M4W 3B8 (✆ 416-921-7376, fax 416-921-1353). **UK** 22-25a Sackville St, London W1X 1DE (✆ 0171-494-1441).

ROMANIA US 342 Madison Ave, Suite 210, New York, NY 10173 (✆ 212-697-6971; fax 212-697-6972). **UK** 83a Marylebone High St, London W1M 3DE (✆ 0171-224-3692).

SLOVAKIA US 10 E 40th St, Suite 3604, New York, NY 10016 (✆ 212-213-3865, fax 212-213-4461).

SLOVENIA US 122 E 42nd St, Suite 3006, New York, NY 10168 (✆ 212-682-5896, fax 212-661-2469).

SPAIN US 666 5th Ave, 35th floor, New York, NY 10022 (✆1-888-OK-SPAIN or 212-265-8822; fax 212-980-1053). **Canada** 2 Bloor St W, 34th Floor, Toronto, ON M4W 3E2

(℗ 416-961-3131). **UK** 57 St James St, London SW1A 1LD
(℗ 0171-499-0901).

SWEDEN For **US**, see entry for Denmark. They do have a
separate fax number, though, at ℗ 212-697-0835. **UK** 11
Montagu Place, London W1H (℗ 0171-724-5868).

SWITZERLAND US 608 5th Ave, New York, NY 10020
(℗ 212-757-5944; fax 212-262-6116). **Canada** 926 The East
Mall, Etobicoke, ON M9B 6K1 (℗ 416-695-2090, fax 416-
695-2774). **UK** Swiss Centre, New Coventry St, London
W1V 8EE (℗ 0171-734-1921).

TURKEY US 821 UN Plaza, New York, NY 10017
(℗ 212-687-2194/2195/2196; fax 212-599-7568).
Canada 360 Albert St, Suite 801, Ottawa, ON K1R 7X7
(℗ 613-230-8654, fax 613-230-3683). **UK** 170-173 Piccadilly,
London W1V (℗ 0171-629-7771).

UNITED KINGDOM US 551 5th Ave, Suite 701,
New York, NY 10176 (℗ 212-986-2200; fax 212-986-1188);
Canada 111 Avenue Rd, Suite 450, Toronto, ON M5R 3J8
(℗ 416-925-2175). **Australia** Midland House, 210 Clarence
St, Sydney, NSW 2000 (℗ 02-267-4555). **New Zealand**
Dilworth Building, Corner Queen and Customs St, Auckland
1, NZ (℗ 09-303-1446)

4 AIRLINES

Aer Lingus in US and Canada, ℗ 1-800-223-6537 or
℗ 212-557-1110. Ireland's national airline.

Aeroflot in US, ℗ 1-800-995-5555; in Canada,
℗ 514-288-2125/2126; in UK, ℗ 0171-355-2233; in Australia,
℗ 02-9233-7911; in New Zealand, ℗ 09-378-0157. The
remnants of the state airline of the USSR.

Air Canada in Canada, call information, ℗ 1-800-555-1212,
for local toll-free number; in US, ℗ 1-800-776-3000.

Air France in US, ℗ 1-800-237-2747; in Canada,
℗ 1-800-667-2747; in UK, ℗ 0181-742-6600; in Australia,
℗ 02-9321-1030; in New Zealand, ℗ 09-303-1229.

Air New Zealand in New Zealand, ✆ 09-366-2424; in Australia, ✆ 02-9223-4666.

Alitalia in US and Canada, ✆ 1-800-223-5730; in UK, ✆ 0171-602-7111; in Australia, ✆ 02-9247-1308; in New Zealand, ✆ 09-379-4457. Good service.

American Airlines in US, ✆ 1-800-433-7300; in Canada, ✆1-800-667-2747. Good Muzak.

Austrian Airlines in US and Canada, ✆ 1-800-843-0002; in UK, ✆ 0171-434-7300.

British Airways in US, ✆ 1-800-247-9297; in Canada in area codes 519, 613, 705 and 807, ✆ 1-800-243-6822, in 416 ✆ 250-0880; in UK, ✆ 0181-759-2525; in Australia, ✆ 02-9258-3300; in New Zealand, ✆ 09-367-7500.

Canadian Airlines in Canada, ✆ 1-800-665-1177; in US, ✆ 1-800-426-7000.

Continental Airlines in US, ✆ 1-800-231-0856; in Canada, ✆ 416-969-5551.

CSA/Czechoslovak Airlines in US, ✆ 212-765-6022; in Canada, ✆ 416-363-3174; in UK, ✆ 0171-255-1898; in Australia, ✆ 02-247-6196.

Delta Airlines in US, ✆ 1-800-241-4141; in Canada, call information, ✆ 1-800-555-1212, for local toll-free number.

Finnair in US, ✆ 1-800-950-5000; in Canada, ✆ 1-800-461-8651; in UK, ✆ 0171-408-1222.

Icelandair in US and Canada, ✆ 1-800-223-5500.

Iberia in US and Canada, ✆ 1-800-772-4642; in UK, ✆ 0181-830-0011. The Spanish national carrier.

KLM in US, ✆ 1-800-374-7747; in Canada, ✆ 1-800-361-5330 or ✆ 416-204-5100; in UK, ✆ 0181-750-9000; in Australia, ✆ 1-800-505-747 or ✆ 02-9231-6333. Royal Dutch Airlines.

LOT Polish Airlines in US, ✆ 1-800-223-0593; in Canada, ✆ 1-800-361-9071 or ✆ 416-236-4242; in UK, ✆ 0171-580-5037.

Lufthansa in US, ✆ 1-800-645-3880; in Canada, ✆ 1-800-563-5954; in UK, ✆ 0345-737-747. Germany's national airline.

Malév Hungarian Airlines in US and Canada, ✆ 1-800-223-6884; in UK, ✆ 0171-439-0577.

Martinair Holland in US, ✆ 1-800-627-8462; in Canada, ✆ 416-364-3672.

Northwest Airlines in US and Canada, ✆ 1-800-447-4747.

Olympic Airways in US and Canada, ✆ 1-800-223-1226 or ✆ 212-838-3600; in UK, ✆ 0171-409-3400. Very friendly; great Greek music while on hold.

QANTAS in Australia, ✆ 008-112-121 or 02-9236-3636; in New Zealand, ✆ 09-303-2506. QANTAS is the major carrier out of Australia and has great service and the most wonderful flight attendants known to man. Hi, Carolyn!

Royal Air Maroc in US, ✆ 212-750-6071; in Canada, ✆ 1-800-361-7508; in UK, ✆ 0171-439-8854.

Sabena in US and Canada, ✆ 1-800-955-2000; in UK, ✆ 0181-780-1444. Belgium's national airline.

SAS (Scandinavian Airlines) in US and Canada, ✆ 1-800-221-2350; in UK, ✆ 0171-465-0123.

Swissair in US, ✆ 1-800-221-4750; in Canada, ✆ 1-800-267-9477; in UK, ✆ 0171-759-1818.

TAP Air Portugal in US and Canada, ✆ 1-800-221-7370 or ✆ 201-344-4490; in UK, ✆ 0171-630-0900.

THY Turkish Airlines in US and Canada, ✆ 1-800-874-8875; in UK, ✆ 0171-499-4499.

Tower Air in US, ✆ 1-800-221-2500. Flies out of the States only.

TWA in US, ✆ 1-800-892-4141; in Canada, ✆ 1-800-221-2000.

United Airlines in US and Canada, ✆ 1-800-538-2929 or ✆ 1-800-241-6522; in UK, ✆ 0181-990-9900; in Australia, ✆ 02-9237-8888; in New Zealand, ✆ 09-307-9500.

US Air in US and Canada, ✆ 1-800-622-1015.

Varig in US, ✆ 1-800-468-2744; in Canada call information, ✆ 1-800-555-1212, for local toll-free number.

Virgin Atlantic Airways in US and Canada, ✆ 1-800-862-8621; in UK, ✆ 01293-562345.

5 DISCOUNT FLIGHT AGENTS AND CONSOLIDATORS

UNITED STATES AND CANADA

Air Courier Association, 191 University Blvd, Suite 300, Denver, CO 80206 (℡ 303-278-8810). Courier flight broker.

Airhitch, 2472 Broadway, Suite 200, New York, NY 10025 (℡ 1-800-326-8009 or 212-864-2000). Standby-seat broker: For a set price, they guarantee to get you on a flight as close to your preferred destination as possible, within a week. Western Europe only.

Council Travel, 205 E 42nd St, New York, NY 10017 (℡ 1-800-2COUNCIL), and branches in many other US cities. Student travel organization. A sister company, Council Charter (℡ 1-800-223-7402), specializes in charter flights to Europe only.

Educational Travel Center, 438 N Frances St, Madison, WI 53703 (℡ 1-800-747-5551). Student/youth discount agent..

Interworld Travel, 800 Douglass Rd, Miami, FL 33134 (℡ 305-443-4929). Consolidator.

Nouvelles Frontières/New Frontiers, 12 E 33rd St, New York, NY 10016 (℡ 1-800-366-6387); 1001 Sherbrook East, Suite 720, Montréal, PQ H2L 1L3 (℡ 514-526-8444); and other branches in LA, San Francisco, and Québec City. French discount travel firm.

Now Voyager, 74 Varick St, Suite 307, New York, NY 10013 (℡ 212-431-1616). Courier flight broker.

STA Travel, 48 E 11th St, New York, NY 10003 (℡ 1-800-777-0112), and many other branches in the US and Canada. Discount airfares and student travel.

TFI Tours International, 34 W 32nd St, New York, NY 10001 (℡ 1-800-745-8000), also in Las Vegas. Consolidator.

Travac, 989 6th Ave, New York NY 10018, and 2601 E Jefferson St, Orlando, FL 32803 (℡ 1-800-872-8800; fax 1-888-872-8327). Consolidator and charter broker. Good service.

Travel CUTS/Voyages Campus, 187 College St, Toronto, ON M5T 1P7 (℡ 416-979-2406), and other branches all over

Canada (mostly on or near university campuses). Student travel specialists, with discounted fares for non-students, too.

UniTravel, 1177 N Warson Rd, St Louis, MO 63132 (© 1-800-325-2222). Consolidator.

BRITAIN

Campus Travel, 52 Grosvenor Gardens, London SW1W 0AG(©0171/730 3402); 541 Bristol Rd, Selly Oak, Birmingham B29 6AU (©0121/414 1848); 61 Ditchling Rd, Brighton BN1 4SD (©01273/570226) 18/8/95; 39 Queen's Rd, Clifton, Bristol BS8 1QE (©0117/929 2494); 5 Emmanuel St, Cambridge CB1 1NE (©01223/324283); 53 Forest Rd, Edinburgh EH1 2QP (©0131/668 3303); 166 Deansgate, Manchester M3 3FE (©0161/833 2046); 105–106 St Aldates, Oxford OX1 1DD (©01865/242067 24/4/95); Student/youth travel specialists, with branches also in YHA shops and on university campuses all over Britain.

Council Travel, 28a Poland St, London W1V 3DB (©0171/437 7767). Flights and student discounts.

Nouvelles Frontières, 11 Blenheim St, London W1Y 9LE (©0171/629 7772).

North South Travel, Moulsham Mill Centre, Parkway, Chelmsford, Essex CM2 7PX (©01245/492882). Friendly, competitive travel agency, offering discounted fares worldwide – profits are used to support projects in the developing world, especially the promotion of sustainable tourism.

STA Travel, 86 Old Brompton Rd, London SW7 3LH, 117 Euston Rd, London NW1 2SX , 38 Store St London WC1 (Worldwide ©0171/ 361 6262; Europe ©0171/ 361 6161); 25 Queens Rd, Bristol BS8 1QE (©0117/929 4399); 38 Sidney St, Cambridge CB2 3HX (©01223/366966); 75 Deansgate, Manchester M3 2BW (©0161/834 0668); 88 Vicar Lane, Leeds LS1 7JH (©0113/244 9212); 36 George St, Oxford OX1 2OJ (©01865/792800); and branches in Birmingham, Canterbury, Cardiff, Coventry, Durham, Glasgow, Loughborough, Nottingham, Warwick and Sheffield. Worldwide specialists in low cost flights and tours for students and under-26s.

Trailfinders, 42–50 3/7/95 Earls Court Rd, London W8 6FT
3/7/95 (✆937 5400); 194 Kensington High St, London, W8 7RG
(✆0171/938 3939); 58 Deansgate, Manchester M3 2FF
(✆0161/839 6969); 254–284 Sauchiehall St, Glasgow G2 3EH
(✆0141/353 2224); 22–24 The Priory, Queensway, Birmingham
B4 6BS (✆0121/236 1234); 48 Corn St, Bristol BS1 1HQ
(✆0117/929 9000). One of the best informed and most efficient
agents.

AUSTRALIA AND NEW ZEALAND

Brisbane Discount Travel, 360 Queen St, Brisbane
(✆ 07-3229-9211).

Budget Travel, 16 Fort St, Auckland (✆ 09-379-2099).

Destinations Unlimited, 3 Milford Rd, Milford, Auckland
(✆ 09-486-1303).

Flight Centres, Circular Quay, Sydney (✆ 02-9241-2422);
Bourke St, Melbourne (03-650-2899); National Bank Towers,
205-225 Queen St, Auckland (✆ 09-309-6171). Other
branches throughout both Australia and New Zealand.

STA Travel, 732 Harris St, Ultimo, Sydney (✆ 02-9212-1255);
Travellers Centre, 10 High St, Auckland (✆ 09-366-6673).
Offices in major cities and university areas across Australia
and New Zealand. Student and under-26 discounts.

6 TRAVEL BOOK AND MAP STORES

The list of bookstores that follows is necessarily very
abbreviated – there must be several hundred bookstores
specializing in travel products in the United States and
Canada. Check your local telephone directory under both
"bookstores" and "maps." Many of those that follow have
catalogs or newsletters that are

worth sending for. If there is a travel bookstore in your area that is not on the list that you feel should be included, please let me know and I'll try to include it in the next edition.

UNITED STATES AND CANADA

Book Passage, 51 Tamal Vista Blvd, Corte Madera, CA 94925; ✆ 1-800-999-7909 for orders, 415-927-0960 for anything else. Huge selection of travel books and maps. Sponsors a nationally recognized travel writers' conference every August. Excellent phone service.

The Complete Traveller, 3207 Fillmore St, San Francisco, CA 92123; ✆ 415-923-1511. Travel books, maps, luggage, and other accessories.

Going Places Map and Travel Bookstores, 3860 University Ave, Madison, WI 53704; ✆ 608-233-1920.

Nations Travel Mall, 500–504 Pier Ave, Hermosa Beach, CA 90254; ✆ 1-800-546-8060 or 310-318-9915, fax 310-318-9115. Books, maps, travel equipment and accessories, plus a travel agency. Ships free anywhere in the US. Excellent phone service.

Open Air Books and Maps, 25 Toronto St, Toronto, ON M5C 2R1; ✆ 416-363-0719.

Phileas Fogg's Books Maps, 87 Stanford Shopping Center, Palo Alto, CA 94304; ✆ 1-800-533-3644 or 413-327-1754, fax 413-329-8017. Books, maps, videos, travel accessories and language materials.

Rand McNally, 150 E 52nd St, New York, NY 10022; ✆ 212-758-7488. 595 Market St, San Francisco, CA 94105; ✆ 415-777-3131. Plus more than twenty stores across the US; call ✆ 1-800-333-0136 (ext 2111) for the address of the nearest. Maps, books, and travel accessories.

Traveler's Bookstore, 22 W 52nd St, New York, NY 10019; ✆ 212-664-0995. Maps, books, and travel accessories.

World Wide Travel Books and Maps, 736A Granville St, Vancouver, BC V6Z 1G3; ✆ 604-687-3320, fax 604-687-5925. Books, maps, and globes.

BRITAIN

Daunt Books, 83 Marylebone High St, London W1
(℃ 0171/224 2295).

National Map Centre, 22–24 Caxton St, London SW1
(℃ 0171/222 4945).

John Smith and Sons, 57–61 St Vincent St, Glasgow G2 5TB
24/8/95 (℃ 0141/221 7472).

Stanfords, 12–14 Long Acre, WC2 (℃ 0171/836 1321); 52
Grosvenor Gardens, London SW1W 0AG; 156 Regent St,
London W1R 5TA.

The Travel Bookshop, 13–15 Blenheim Crescent, London
W11 2EE (℃ 0171/229 5260).

AUSTRALIA

The Map Shop, 16a Peel St, Adelaide: (℃ 08/8231 2033)
Bowyangs, 372 Little Burke St, Melbourne: (℃ 03/9670 4383).
Perth Map Centre, 891 Hay St, Perth: (℃ 09/9322 5733).
Travel Bookshop, 20 Bridge St, Sydney: (℃ 02/9241 3554).

NEW ZEALAND

Specialty Maps, 58 Albert St, Auckland: (℃ 09/307 2217).

7 TRAVEL EQUIPMENT SUPPLIERS

All of the equipment companies listed below sell products
which may be of interest to the traveler. I have bought
from all the North American ones and have had good
experiences. Overseas buyers will probably not be able to
use the 800 numbers, so try faxing for catalogs. Aussies
remember: It is much cheaper to buy this type of travel
equipment in the States than in Australia.

UNITED STATES AND CANADA

Campmoor, PO Box 700, Saddle River, NJ 07458-0700;
℃ 1-800-226-7667 or 201-825-8300; fax 1-800-230-2153 or

201-825-0274. This place sells outdoor gear, specializing in clothing and, not surprisingly, camping gear.

The North Face, Nine stores throughout the US, selling high-end camping gear and clothing. Call ℂ 1-800-362-4963 for the store closest to you, or try 510-618-3500; fax 510-618-3532.

Recreational Equipment, Inc, Sumner, WA 98352-0001; ℂ 1-800-426-4840 or 206-891-2500; fax 206-891-2523. A huge mail-order company that also has about sixty retail stores, mainly in the west. Call to see if there is a store in your area or for a catalog. This company is good for outdoor equipment and clothes.

Sierra Trading Post, 5025 Campstool Rd, Cheyenne, WY 82007–1802; ℂ 1-800-713-4534; fax 1-800-378-8946 or 307-775-8089. This company specializes in clothing and shoes, but has good deals on some of the smaller pieces of equipment, such as sunglasses.

Travel Smith, 3140 Kerner Blvd, San Rafael, CA 94901; ℂ 1-800-950-1600 or 415-455-8050, fax 415-455-0329. Although this operation has some yuppie-looking products, some of their prices are decent, and the catalog is worth a look.

BRITAIN

YHA Adventure Shop, 14 Southampton St, London WC2E 7HA (ℂ 0171-836 8541). Main branch of Britain's best outdoor equipment supplier.

AUSTRALIA

A-Roving, 102 Elizabeth St, Melbourne; ℂ 654-7264.

Mountain Designs, 105 Albert St, Brisbane; ℂ 221-6756.

Mtn Equipment Pty, Ltd, 491 Kent St, Sydney, NSW 2000; ℂ 264-5888.

Paddy Pallin, 507 Kent St, Sydney, NSW 2000; ℂ 264-2685 or ℂ 261-8572. Also, 360 Lt Bourke St, Melbourne; ℂ 670-4845.

8 INSURANCE PROVIDERS

Take a good long look at all the restrictions and requirements involved with an insurance policy before buying one. The costs and coverages provided by the companies listed here vary widely, though all are very expensive. For two or three months' coverage, expect to pay $150-300. Be aware that "high risk" activities may not be included or may cost extra. The best procedure if you think you need this kind of insurance is to send away for as much information as possible, and actually read all of the pages of fine print you will receive. In addition to the companies listed here, most travel agents offer insurance: Again, don't just accept what they offer without checking it out first. Remember, if you get an international student, youth, or teacher card, you get insurance that may be as good as that provided by the companies listed; check, too, any health or household insurance you already hold to see if that covers you.

UNITED STATES AND CANADA

Travel Assistance International, ✆ 1-800-821-2828, fax 202-828-5896. This company provides medical coverage, as well as trip and luggage insurance.

Travel Insured International, Inc ✆ 1-800-243-3174, fax 203-528-8005.

Access America ✆ 1-800-284-8300.

Carefree Travel Insurance ✆ 1-800-323-3149.

Council Travel ✆ 1-800-2-council.

Travel Guard ✆ 1-800-826-1300.

BRITAIN

Columbus Travel Insurance ✆ 0171-375-0011.

Endsleigh Insurance ✆ 0171-436-4451.

Marcus Hearn & Co ✆ 0171-739-3444.

AUSTRALIA

CIC Insurance ✆ 9202-8000.

9 ONLINE TRAVEL RESOURCES

In addition to consulting books, travel agents, airlines, rail companies and so on, you can find a great deal of useful travel information on the World Wide Web. Some are more flash than cash, but the ones mentioned in this section are all worth a look. A quick net search will reveal many more.

Adventurous Traveler Bookstore

http://www.gorp.com/atbook.html

Guidebooks, maps, and videos to help you on your way.

Book Passage

http://www.Bookpassage.com

Books of every kind, including a huge travel selection.

CIA World Factbook

http://www.odci.gov/cia/publications/pubs.html

An encyclopedic summary of every country's essential statistics: geographical boundaries, international disputes, climate, geography, economic indicators, demographics, government, communications, and defense.

City.Net http://www.city.net/

A regionally sorted digest of links to community, geopolitical, and tourist information from all around the globe.

European Railways Information

http://mercurio.iet.unipi.it/home.html

Timetables, news, locomotive pictures, and related links.

GNN Travel Resource Center
http://www.gnn.com/gnn/meta/
travel/index.html. GNN has an excellent travel section, with a
huge array of links around the Web from its "Travelers'
Reading Room."

International Student Travel Confederation
http://www.istc.org
Find out where to get an international student identity card
and what it's good for.

Internet Guide to Hosteling
http://www.webcom.com/hostels
Gives details and recommendations for hostels all over
Europe.

Internet Travel Network http://www.itn.net
Real-time airline reservation system, also with reservation
access for hotels and car rentals, and information from fellow
world travelers.

Lonely Planet Guidebooks http://www.lonelyplanet.com
More global than European, but inspiring: check out the
Postcards from Abroad, for proof that it's all possible.

Paris http://www.paris.org/
Virtual tour of popular museums, cafés, monuments, stores,
rail systems, educational institutions, and other attractions. In
English or French.

RailServer http://rail.rz.uni-karlsruhe.de/rail/english.html
Extensive European rail travel information,, with an emphasis
on Germany, providing schedules, pictures, prices and
discounts, plus hints and links to sites.

Rough Guides http://roughguides.com/
Rough Guides' home page includes an A–Z of titles, with
excerpts, updates and complete menu readers for France and
Italy to download. Rough Guides' joint venture with
HotWired (at http://www.hotwired.com/rough) allows you to
browse titles from the series online, including much of the
Rough Guide to Europe.

Time Out http://www.timeout.co.uk
Time Out, London's weekly listings guide, offers a bonanza of

information on how to pass the time in London, Amsterdam, Berlin, Madrid, Paris, and Prague.

Travel Channel Online http://www.travelchannel.com
The cable tv channel on the web, spotlighting different destinations around the globe, along with discussion forums, photos, and the like.

The Virtual Tourist http://wings.buffalo.edu/world/
Click on the atlas to zoom into the region of your choice: The project aims to link with all Web travel info.

World's Largest Subway Map http://metro.jussieu.fr:10001/
Plan your route across London on the Underground or Paris by Metro, plus every other major subway system in the world.

10 LANGUAGES

In Germany, Scandinavia, and especially The Netherlands and Switzerland, many people, particularly the young, speak reasonable English. It's polite, however, to know at least a few very basic words and phrases wherever you happen to be, which is why we've included the following chart. A smattering of French or German is handy everywhere as a common language if English fails.

Pocket dictionaries and language courses for most European languages can easily be bought in the countries where they are spoken, and usually at home, too. There is also a wide assortment of language phrasebooks from which to choose. Check your local bookstore.

English	Bulgarian	Czech	Danish
Yes	Da	Ano	Ja
No	Ne	Ne	Nej
Please	Molya	Prosím	Vaerså venlig
Thank you	Blagodarya	Děkuju	Tak
Hello/Good day	Dobăr den	Dobry den/ahoj	Goddag
Goodbye	Dovizhdane	Na shledanou	Farvel
Excuse me	Izvinyavaïte	Promiňte	Undskyld
Where	Kude	Kde	Hvor
When	Koga	Kdy	Hvornår
How	Kak	Jak	Hvordan
Left	Lyavo	Vlevo	Venstre
Right	Dyasno	Vpravo	Højre
Large	Golyama	Velký	Stor
Small	Malko	Maly	Lille
Good	Dobro	Dobry	God
Bad	Plosho	Spatny	Dårlig
Near	Blizo	Blízko	Naer
Far	Daleche	Daleko	Fjern
Cheap	Eftino	Levný	Billig
Expensive	Skupo	Drahý	Dyr
Open	Otvoreno	Otevřeno	Åben
Closed	Zatvoreno	Zavřeno	Lukket
Today	Dnes	Dnes	I dag
Yesterday	Vechera	Včera	I går
Tomorrow	Utre	Zítra	I morgen
Day	Den	Den	Dag
Week	Sedmitza	Tyden	Uge
Month	Mesetz	Mesíc	Måned
Year	Godina	Rok	År
How much is....?	Kolko...?	Kolík stojí...?	Hvor koster er...?
What time is it?	Kolko e chasut?	Kolík je hodin?	Hvad er klokken?
Where is...?	Kude e	Kde je...?	Hvor er...?
I don't understand	Ne vi razbiram	Nerozumím	Jeg forstår ikke
Do you speak English?	Govorite li Angliski?	Miuvíte Anglicky?	Taler de Engelsk?
Please write it down	Molya napishete go	Prosím, napište to	Vaer venlig at skrive det

One	Edin	Jeden	En
Two	Dve	Dva	To
Three	Tri	Tri	Tre
Four	Chetiri	Ctyri	Fire
Five	Pet	Pet	Fem
Six	Shest	Sest	Seks
Seven	Sedem	Sedm	Syv
Eight	Osem	Osum	Otte
Nine	Devet	Devet	Ni
Ten	Deset	Deset	Ti

English	Dutch	Estonian	Finnish
Yes	Ja	Jaa	Kyllä
No	Nee	Ei	Ei
Please	Alstublieft	Palun	Olkaa hyvä
Thank you	Dank u/Bedankt	Tänan	Kiitos
Hello/Good day	Dag	Tere	Hyvää
Goodbye	Tot ziens	Head aega	Hyvästi
Excuse me	Pardon	Vabandage	Anteeksi
Where	Waar	Kus	Missä
When	Wanneer	Millal	Milloin
How	Hoe	Kuidas	Kuinka
Left	Links	Vasak	Vasen
Right	Rechts	Parem	Oikea
Large	Groot	Suur	Suuri
Small	Klein	Väike	Pieni
Good	Goed	Hea	Hyvä
Bad	Slecht	Halb	Paha
Near	Dichtbij	Lähedal	Lähellä
Far	Ver	Kaugel	Kaukana
Cheap	Goedkoop	Odav	Halpa
Expensive	Duur	Kallis	Kallis
Open	Open	Avatud	Avoin
Closed	Dicht	Suletud	Suljettu
Today	Vandaag	Täna	Tänään
Yesterday	Gisteren	Eile	Eilen
Tomorrow	Morgen	Homme	Huomenna
Day	Dag	Päev	Päivä
Week	Week	Nädal	Viikko
Month	Maand	Kuu	Kuukausi
Year	Jaar	Aasta	Vuosi
How much is....?	Wat kost....?	Kui palju maksab ...?	Kuinka paljon on ...?
What time is it?	Hoe laat is het?	Mis kell praegu on?	Paljonko kello on?
Where is...?	Waar is...?	Kus on ...?	Missä on...?
I don't understand	Ik begrijp het niet	Ma ei saa aru	En ymmärrä
Do you speak English?	Spreekt u Engels?	Kas te räägite inglise keelt?	Puhutteko Englantia?
Please write it down	Wilt u het opschrijven, alstublieft	Palun kirjutage see üles.	Olkaa hyvä ja kiarjoittakaa se

One	Een	Üks	Yksi
Two	Twee	Tkaks	Kaksi
Three	Drie	Kolm	Kolme
Four	Vier	Neli	Neljä
Five	Vijf	Viis	Viisi
Six	Zes	Kuus	Kuusi
Seven	Zeven	Seitse	Seitsemän
Eight	Acht	Kaheksa	Kahdeksan
Nine	Negen	Üheksa	Yhdeksän
Ten	Tien	Kümme	Kymmenen

English	French	German	Greek
Yes	Oui	Ja	Néh
No	Non	Nein	Óhi
Please	S'il vous plaît	Bitte	Parakaló
Thank you	Merci	Danke	Efharistó
Hello/Good day	Bonjour	Güten Tag	Adío
Goodbye	Au revoir	Auf Wiedersehen	Hérete
Excuse me	Pardon	Entschuldigen Sie, bitte	Signómi
Where	Où	Wo	Pou
When	Quand	Wann	Póte
How	Comment	Wie	Pos
Left	Gauche	Links	Aristerá
Right	Droite	Rechts	Dheksiá
Large	Grand	Gross	Megálo
Small	Petit	Klein	Mikró
Good	Bon	Gut	Kaló
Bad	Mauvais	Schlecht	Kakó
Near	Près	Nah	Kondá
Far	Loin	Weit	Makriá
Cheap	Bon marché	Billig	Fthinós
Expensive	Cher	Teuer	Akrivós
Open	Ouvert	Offen	Aniktós
Closed	Fermé	Geschlossen	Klistós
Today	Aujourd'hui	Heute	Símera
Yesterday	Hier	Gestern	Khthés
Tomorrow	Demain	Morgen	Ávrio
Day	Jour	Tag	Méra
Week	Semaine	Woche	Iméra
Month	Mois	Monat	Evdomáda
Year	Année	Jahr	Chrónos
How much is....?	Combien est...?	Wieviel kostet....?	Póso káni...?
What time is it?	Quelle heure est-il?	Wieviel Uhr ist es?	Ti óra inai...?
Where is...?	Où est...?	Wo ist...?	Pou íne...?
I don't understand	Je ne comprends pas	Ich verstehe nicht	Dhen katalavéno
Do you speak English?	Parlez-vous anglais?	Sprechen Sie Englisch?	Ksérite Angliká?
Please write it down	Veuillez me l'écrire	Bitte schreiben Sie es	Parakaló grápiste to

One	Un	Eins	Éna
Two	Deux	Zwei	Dhío
Three	Trois	Drei	Tría
Four	Quatre	Vier	Téseres
Five	Cinq	Fünf	Pénde
Six	Six	Sechs	Éksi
Seven	Sept	Sieben	Eftá
Eight	Huit	Acht	Októ
Nine	Neuf	Neun	Enyá
Ten	Dix	Zehn	Dhéka

English	Hungarian	Italian	Latvian
Yes	Igen	Si	Jā
No	Nem	No	Nē
Please	Kérem	Per favore	Lūdzu
Thank you	Köszönöm	Grazie	Paldies
Hello/Good day	Jó napot	Ciao/buon giorno	Labdien
Goodbye	Viszontlá-tásta	Ciao/arriverderci	Uz redzēšanos
Excuse me	Bocsánat	Mi scusi/prego	Atvainojiet
Where	Hol	Dove	Kur
When	Mikor	Quando	Kad
How	Hogyan	Come	Cik
Left	Balra	Sinistra	Kreisi
Right	Jobbra	Destra	Labi
Large	Nagy	Grande	Liels
Small	Kicsi	Piccolo	Mazs
Good	Jó	Buono	Labs
Bad	Rossz	Cattivo	Slikts
Near	Közel	Vicino	Tuvs
Far	Távol	Lontano	Tāls
Cheap	Olcsó	Buon mercato	Lēts
Expensive	Drága	Caro	Dārgs
Open	Nyitva	Aperto	Atvērts
Closed	Zárva	Chiuso	Slēgts
Today	Ma	Oggi	Šodien
Yesterday	Tegnap	Ieri	Vakar
Tomorrow	Holnap	Domani	Rīt
Day	Nap	Giorno	Diena
Week	Hét	Settimana	Bedeka
Month	Hónap	Mese	Menesis
Year	Ev	Anno	Gads
How much is....?	Mennyibe Kerül...?	Quanto è...?	Cik tas maksā ...?
What time is it?	Hány óra?	Che ore sono?	Cik ir pulkstenis?
Where is...?	Hol van?	Dov'è...?	Kur ir ...?
I don't understand	Nem értem	Non ho capito	Es nesaprotu
Do you speak English?	Beszél Angolul?	Parla Inglese?	Vai jūs runājat Angliski?
Please write it down	Legyen szives, irja le	Lo scriva, per favore	Lūdzu uzrakstiet
One	Egy	Uno	Viens
Two	Kettö	Due	Divi
Three	Három	Tre	Trīs
Four	Négy	Quattro	C&etri
Five	Ot	Cinque	Pieci
Six	Hayt	Sei	Seši
Seven	Hét	Sette	Septiņi
Eight	Nyolc	Otto	Astoņi
Nine	Kilenc	Nove	Deviņi
Ten	Tíz	Dieci	Desmit

English	Lithuanian	Norwegian	Polish
Yes	Taip	Ja	Tak
No	Ne	Nei	Nie
Please	Prašau	Vaer så god	Prosze
Thank you	Ačiu	Takk	Dziekuje
Hello/Good day	Labas	God dag	Dzien dobry
Goodbye	Viso gero	Adjø	Do widzenia
Excuse me	Atsiprašau	Unnskyld	Przepraszam
Where	Kur	Hvor	Gdzie
When	Kada	Når	Kiedy
How	Kaip	Hvordan	Jak
Left	Kairė	Venstre	Na lewo
Right	Dešinė	Høyre	Na prawo
Large	Didelis	Stor	Wielki
Small	Mažas	Liten	Maly
Good	Geras	God	Dobry
Bad	Blogas	Dårlig	Zly
Near	Artimas	I naerheten	Blisko
Far	Tolimas	Langt Borte	Daleko
Cheap	Pigus	Billig	Tani
Expensive	Brangus	Dyr	Drogi
Open	Atidarytas	Åpen	Otwarty
Closed	Uždarytas	Lukket	Zamknięty
Today	Šiandien	I dag	Dzisiaj
Yesterday	Vakar	I går	Wczoraj
Tomorrow	Rytdiena	I morgen	Jutro
Day	Diena	Dag	Dzień
Week	Savaitė	Uke	Tydzień
Month	Mėnuo	Måned	Miesiąc
Year	Metai	År	Rok
How much is....?	Kiek kainuoja ...?	Hvor mye er...?	Lle Losztuje...?
What time is it?	Kiek valandų?	Hvor mange er klokken?	Która godzina?
Where is...?	Kur yra ...?	Hvor er...?	Gdzie jest . . . ?
I don't understand	Nesuprantu	Jeg forstår ikke	Nie rozemiem
Do you speak English?	Ar jųs kalbate angliškai?	Snakker de Englesk?	Pani mówi po Angielsku?
Please write it down	Prašau užrašyti	Vennligst skriv det ned	Proszę to napisać

One	Vienas	En	Jeden
Two	Du/dvi	To	Dwa
Three	Trys	Tre	Trzy
Four	Keturi	Fire	Cztery
Five	Penki	Fem	Piec
Six	Šeši	Seks	Szesc
Seven	Septyni	Sju	Siedem
Eight	Aštuoni	Åtte	Osiem
Nine	Devyni	Ni	Dziewiec
Ten	Dešimt	Ti	Dziesiec

English	Portuguese	Romanian	Russian
Yes	Sim	Da	Da
No	Não	Nu	Net
Please	Por favor	Vă rog	Pazhahlsta
Thank you	Obrigado	Mulțumesc	Spasíbo
Hello/Good day	Olá	Salut/Buna ziua	Pree-vyet (formal zdrávstvuyte)
Goodbye	Adeus	La revedere	Do svidániya
Excuse me	Desculpe	Permiteți-mi	Pozháluysta
Where	Onde	Unde	Gde
When	Quando	Cînd	Kogdá
How	Como	Cum	Kak
Left	Esquerda	Stînga	Nalévo
Right	Direita	Dreapta	Naprávo
Large	Grande	Mare	Bolshóy
Small	Pequeno	Mic	Málenkiy
Good	Bom	Bun/Bîne	Khoróshiy
Bad	Mau	Rău	Plokhóy
Near	Perto	Apropriat	Bleezkuh
Far	Longe	Departe	Da-lyiko
Cheap	Barato	Ieftin	Dyi-shovee
Expensive	Caro	Scump	Daragoy
Open	Aberto	Închis	Otkrýto
Closed	Fechado	Deschis	Zakrýto
Today	Hoje	Azi	Syivo-dnya
Yesterday	Ontem	Ieri	Vcherá
Tomorrow	Amanhã	Mîine	Závtra
Day	Dia	Zi	Dyin
Week	Semana	Săptămînă	Nyi-dyel-ya
Month	Mês	Lună	Mye-syats
Year	Ano	An	Got
How much is....?	Quanto e... ?	Cît costa...?	Skólko stóit?
What time is it?	Que horas sao?	Ce ora este?	Katoree chass?
Where is...?	Onde é...?	Unde este...?	Gde.....?
I don't understand	Não comprendo	Nu înteleg	Ya ne ponimáyu
Do you speak English?	Fala Inglés?	Vorbiți Englezeste?	Vy govoríte po-anglíyski?
Please write it down	Escreva-mo, por favor	Vă rog scrieți	Zapishíte éto pozháluysta (means could you write it down?)
One	Um	Unu	Odín
Two	Dois	Doi	Dva
Three	Três	Trei	Tri
Four	Quatro	Patru	Chetýre
Five	Cinco	Cinci	Pyat
Six	Seis	Sase	Shest
Seven	Sete	Sapte	Sem
Eight	Oito	Opt	Vósem
Nine	Nove	Noua	Dévyat
Ten	Dez	Zece	Désyat

English	Spanish	Swedish	Turkish
Yes	Si	Ja	Evet
No	No	Nej	Yok
Please	Por favor	Var så god	Lütfen
Thank you	Gracias	Tack	Tesekkür ederim
Hello/Good day	Holá	Hej	Merhaba
Goodbye	Adíos	Adjö	Allahaismarladik
Excuse me	Con permiso	Ursäkta mig	Pardon
Where	Dónde	Var	. . . nerede
When	Cuándo	När	Ne zaman
How	Cómo	Hur	Nas f
Left	Izquierda	Vänster	Sol
Right	Derecha	Höger	Sag
Large	Gran	Stor	Büyuk
Small	Pequeno	Liten	Kücük
Good	Buen	Bra	Iyi
Bad	Mal	Dalig	Kötü
Near	Próximo	Nära	Yakin
Far	Lejos	Avlägsen	Uzak
Cheap	Barato	Billig	Ucuz
Expensive	Caro	Dyr	Pahal f
Open	Abierto	Üppen	Aç k
Closed	Cerrado	Stängd	Kapal f
Today	Hoy	I dag	Bugün
Yesterday	Ayer	I går	Dün
Tomorrow	Mañana	I morgon	Yarin
Day	Día	Dag	Gün
Week	Semana	Vecka	Hafta
Month	Mes	Månad	Ay
Year	Año	Är	Sene
How much is....?	Cuánto costa...?	Vad kostar det...?	Ne kadar...?
What time is it?	Tiene la hora?	Hur mycket är klockan?	Saatiniz var mi?
Where is...?	Dónde estar...?	Var är...?	Nerede...?
I don't understand	No entiendo	Jag förstår int	Anlamadim
Do you speak English?	Habla Inglés?	Talar ni Engelska?	Ingilizce Biliyormusunuz?
Please write it down	Escríbamelo, por favor?	Skulle ni kunna skriva det?	Onu yazarm s ñ f
One	Un	Ett	Bir
Two	Dos	Två	Iki
Three	Tres	Tre	Uç
Four	Cuatro	Fyra	Dört
Five	Cinco	Fem	Bes
Six	Seis	Sex	Alti
Seven	Siete	Sju	Yedi
Eight	Ocho	Ätta	Sekiz
Nine	Nueve	Nio	Dokuz
Ten	Diez	Tio	On

11 FINAL CHECKLIST

DOCUMENTS

PASSPORT
ISIC CARD (OR OTHER YOUTH/TEACHER ID)
CREDIT CARD
TRAIN PASS
MAPS
PASSPORT COPY
CREDIT CARD COPIES (LEAVE AT HOME)
TRAIN TIMETABLE
HOSTEL CARD
HOSTELING GUIDE AND MAP
EXTRA PASSPORT-SIZED PHOTOS
JOURNAL

ESSENTIALS

BACKPACK
DAYPACK
BACKPACK LOCKS
MONEY BELT
SLEEP SACK
CLOTHES/SHOES
CLOCK/WATCH
TOWEL
FIRST-AID KIT
SEWING/REPAIR KIT
SUN SCREEN/LIP BALM
SUNGLASSES
FLASHLIGHT
BUG DOPE/HEAD NET
BACKPACK COVER
CAMERA/FILM/BATTERY
PADLOCK AND CHAIN

RAIN GEAR/UMBRELLA

SWISS ARMY KNIFE

CALCULATOR

LAUNDRY BAGS

TOILET PAPER

BATHROOM KIT

CONTACT LENSES/CLEANER

GLASSES

EARPLUGS

DRAIN PLUG

GUIDEBOOK(S)

OPTIONAL

SLEEPING BAG

COOKING GEAR

CLOTHESPINS/LINE

TENT

GROUND PAD

STOVE

COMPASS

WHISTLE

WALKMAN/TAPES

PLAYING CARDS

PICTURES AND POSTCARDS

direct orders from

Amsterdam	1-85828-218-7	UK£8.99	US$14.95	CAN$19.99
Andalucia	1-85828-219-5	9.99	16.95	22.99
Australia	1-85828-220-9	13.99	21.95	29.99
Bali	1-85828-134-2	8.99	14.95	19.99
Barcelona	1-85828-221-7	8.99	14.95	19.99
Berlin	1-85828-129-6	8.99	14.95	19.99
Belgium & Luxembourg	1-85828-222-5	10.99	17.95	23.99
Brazil	1-85828-102-4	9.99	15.95	19.99
Britain	1-85828-208-X	12.99	19.95	25.99
Brittany & Normandy	1-85828-224-1	9.99	16.95	22.99
Bulgaria	1-85828-183-0	9.99	16.95	22.99
California	1-85828-181-4	10.99	16.95	22.99
Canada	1-85828-130-X	10.99	14.95	19.99
China	1-85828-225-X	15.99	24.95	32.99
Corfu	1-85828-226-8	8.99	14.95	19.99
Corsica	1-85828-227-6	9.99	16.95	22.99
Costa Rica	1-85828-136-9	9.99	15.95	21.99
Crete	1-85828-132-6	8.99	14.95	18.99
Cyprus	1-85828-182-2	9.99	16.95	22.99
Czech & Slovak Republics	1-85828-121-0	9.99	16.95	22.99
Egypt	1-85828-188-1	10.99	17.95	23.99
Europe	1-85828-159-8	14.99	19.95	25.99
England	1-85828-160-1	10.99	17.95	23.99
First Time Europe	1-85828-270-5	7.99	9.95	12.99
Florida	1-85828-184-4	10.99	16.95	22.99
France	1-85828-228-4	12.99	19.95	25.99
Germany	1-85828-128-8	11.99	17.95	23.99
Goa	1-85828-275-6	8.99	14.95	19.99
Greece	1-85828-131-8	9.99	16.95	20.99
Greek Islands	1-85828-163-6	8.99	14.95	19.99
Guatemala	1-85828-189-X	10.99	16.95	22.99
Hawaii: Big Island	1-85828-158-X	8.99	12.95	16.99
Hawaii	1-85828-206-3	10.99	16.95	22.99
Holland	1-85828-229-2	10.99	17.95	23.99
Hong Kong	1-85828-187-3	8.99	14.95	19.99
Hungary	1-85828-123-7	8.99	14.95	19.99
India	1-85828-200-4	14.99	23.95	31.99
Ireland	1-85828-179-2	10.99	17.95	23.99
Italy	1-85828-167-9	12.99	19.95	25.99
Jamaica	1-85828-230-6	9.99	16.95	22.99
Kenya	1-85828-192-X	11.99	18.95	24.99
London	1-85828-231-4	9.99	15.95	21.99
Mallorca & Menorca	1-85828-165-2	8.99	14.95	19.99
Malaysia, Singapore & Brunei	1-85828-232-2	11.99	18.95	24.99
Mexico	1-85828-044-3	10.99	16.95	22.99
Morocco	1-85828-040-0	9.99	16.95	21.99
Moscow	1-85828-118-0	8.99	14.95	19.99
Nepal	1-85828-190-3	10.99	17.95	23.99
New York	1-85828-171-7	9.99	15.95	21.99
Norway	1-85828-234-9	10.99	17.95	23.99
Pacific Northwest	1-85828-092-3	9.99	14.95	19.99

In the UK, Rough Guides are available from all good bookstores, but can be obtained from Penguin by contacting: Penguin Direct, Penguin Books Ltd, Bath Road, Harmondsworth, West Drayton, Middlesex UB7 0DA; or telephone the credit line on 0181-899 4036 (9am–5pm) and ask for Penguin Direct. Visa and Access accepted. Delivery will normally be within 14 working days. Penguin Direct ordering facilities are only available in the UK and the USA. The availability and published prices quoted are correct at the time of going to press but are subject to alteration without prior notice.

around the world

Paris	1-85828-235-7	8.99	14.95	19.99
Poland	1-85828-168-7	10.99	17.95	23.99
Portugal	1-85828-180-6	9.99	16.95	22.99
Prague	1-85828-122-9	8.99	14.95	19.99
Provence	1-85828-127-X	9.99	16.95	22.99
Pyrenees	1-85828-093-1	8.99	15.95	19.99
Rhodes & the Dodecanese	1-85828-120-2	8.99	14.95	19.99
Romania	1-85828-097-4	9.99	15.95	21.99
San Francisco	1-85828-185-7	8.99	14.95	19.99
Scandinavia	1-85828-236-5	12.99	20.95	27.99
Scotland	1-85828-166-0	9.99	16.95	22.99
Sicily	1-85828-178-4	9.99	16.95	22.99
Singapore	1-85828-135-0	8.99	14.95	19.99
Soutwest USA	1-85828-239-X	10.99	16.95	22.99
Spain	1-85828-240-3	11.99	18.95	24.99
St Petersburg	1-85828-133-4	8.99	14.95	19.99
Sweden	1-85828-241-1	10.99	17.95	23.99
Thailand	1-85828-140-7	10.99	17.95	24.99
Tunisia	1-85828-139-3	10.99	17.95	24.99
Turkey	1-85828-242-X	12.99	19.95	25.99
Tuscany & Umbria	1-85828-243-8	10.99	17.95	23.99
USA	1-85828-161-X	14.99	19.95	25.99
Venice	1-85828-170-9	8.99	14.95	19.99
Vietnam	1-85828-191-1	9.99	15.95	21.99
Wales	1-85828-245-4	10.99	17.95	23.99
Washington DC	1-85828-246-2	8.99	14.95	19.99
West Africa	1-85828-101-6	15.99	24.95	34.99
More Women Travel	1-85828-098-2	10.99	16.95	22.99
Zimbabwe & Botswana	1-85828-186-5	11.99	18.95	24.99
Phrasebooks				
Czech	1-85828-148-2	3.50	5.00	7.00
French	1-85828-144-X	3.50	5.00	7.00
German	1-85828-146-6	3.50	5.00	7.00
Greek	1-85828-145-8	3.50	5.00	7.00
Italian	1-85828-143-1	3.50	5.00	7.00
Mexican	1-85828-176-8	3.50	5.00	7.00
Portuguese	1-85828-175-X	3.50	5.00	7.00
Polish	1-85828-174-1	3.50	5.00	7.00
Spanish	1-85828-147-4	3.50	5.00	7.00
Thai	1-85828-177-6	3.50	5.00	7.00
Turkish	1-85828-173-3	3.50	5.00	7.00
Vietnamese	1-85828-172-5	3.50	5.00	7.00
Reference				
Classical Music	1-85828-113-X	12.99	19.95	25.99
European Football	1-85828-256-X	14.99	23.95	31.99
Internet	1-85828-198-9	5.00	8.00	10.00
Jazz	1-85828-137-7	16.99	24.95	34.99
Opera	1-85828-138-5	16.99	24.95	34.99
Reggae	1-85828-247-0	12.99	19.95	25.99
Rock	1-85828-201-2	17.99	26.95	35.00
World Music	1-85828-017-6	16.99	22.95	29.99

In the USA, or for international orders, charge your order by Master Card or Visa (US$15.00 minimum order): call 1-800-253-6476; or send orders, with complete name, address and zip code, and list price, plus $2.00 shipping and handling per order to: Consumer Sales, Penguin USA, PO Box 999 – Dept #17109, Bergenfield, NJ 07621. No COD. Prepay foreign orders by international money order, a cheque drawn on a US bank, or US currency. No postage stamps are accepted. All orders are subject to stock availability at the time they are processed. Refunds will be made for books not available at that time. Please allow a minimum of four weeks for delivery.

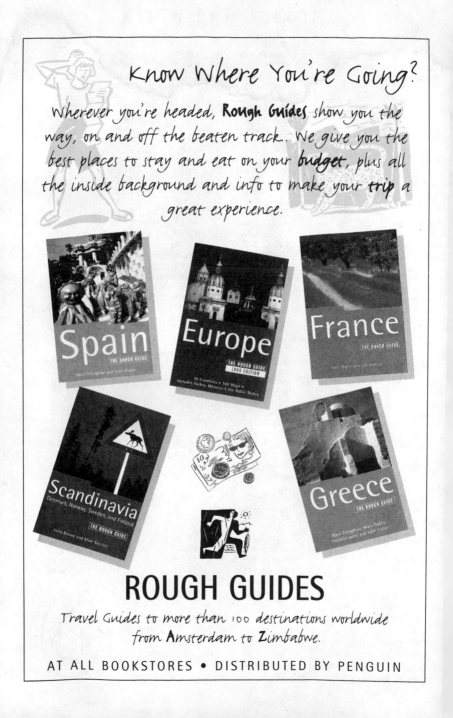

Know Where You're Going?

Wherever you're headed, **Rough Guides** show you the way, on and off the beaten track. We give you the best places to stay and eat on your **budget**, plus all the inside background and info to make your **trip** a great experience.

ROUGH GUIDES

Travel Guides to more than 100 destinations worldwide from **A**msterdam to **Z**imbabwe.

AT ALL BOOKSTORES • DISTRIBUTED BY PENGUIN

IF KNOWLEDGE IS POWER,
THIS ROUGH GUIDE IS A POCKET-SIZED BATTERING RAM

Written in plain English, with no hint of jargon, the Rough Guide to the Internet will make you an Internet guru in the shortest possible time. It cuts through the hype and makes all others look like nerdy textbooks

ROUGH GUIDES ON THE WEB

Visit our website www.roughguides.com for news about the latest books, online travel guides and updates, and the full text of our Rough Guide to Rock.

AT ALL BOOKSTORES • DISTRIBUTED BY PENGUIN

¿Qué pasa?

BRAND NEW ROUGH GUIDES PHRASEBOOKS!

Rough Guide Phrasebooks represent a complete shakeup of the phrasebook format.

Handy and pocket sized, they work like a dictionary to get you straight to the point. With clear guidelines on pronunciation, dialogues for typical situations, and tips on cultural issues, they'll have you speaking the language quicker than any other phrasebook.

Now available
Czech, French, German, Greek, Hindi, Indonesian, Italian, Mandarin, Mexican Spanish, Polish, Portuguese, Russian, Spanish, Thai, Turkish, Vietnamese

Good Vibrations!

ON PAPER AND ONLINE!

Visit Rough Guides' website www.roughguides.com for news
about the latest books, online travel guides and updates, and
the full text of our Rough Guide to Rock.

AT ALL BOOKSTORES • DISTRIBUTED BY PENGUIN

student and youth travel...

Look around...

...Campus Travel makes *sense*

- plane, boat and train fares

- round-the-world flights

- rail & coach passes

- worldwide accommodation

- adventure tours

- travel insurance

- student & youth discount cards

WORLDWIDE
0171 730 8111

EUROPE
0171 730 3402

N. AMERICA
0171 730 2101

52 Grosvenor Gardens opp. Victoria ⊖
Mon, Tues, Weds, Fri 0900-1800; Thurs 0900-2000; Sat 1000-1700; Sun 1000-1500

STANFORDS
TRAVEL BOOKSTORE AT VICTORIA TRAVEL

Or visit any of our other 4 London branches

YHA ADVENTURE SHOPS
14 Southampton St. Covent Gdn ⊖
0171 836 3343

YHA ADVENTURE SHOP
Kensington High St. Ken High St ⊖

STUDENT UNION
UCL Union, 25 Gordon Street, Euston ⊖

STUDENT UNION
South Bank University, Elephant & Castle ⊖

Campus TRAVEL

student & youth travel
www.campustravel.co.uk/